The Art of Curating Worship

I have heard many question our current worship vocabulary and cry out for a new language that helps us better reflect the glory of God. Mark Pierson offers a new approach to leading worship and without using elitist language or ideas that are bound to one particular style. If you are a pastor, musician, technician, artist, VJ, volunteer or anyone involved in leading worship gatherings, this book is a must read. —**Stephen Proctor, worshipvj.com**

Mark Pierson gifts the worshiping Church with something rare indeed: original thought. *The Art of Curating Worship* is a brave new dimension of questions, perspective, and worship practice. —**Sally Morgenthaler, author,** *Worship Evangelism*

Mark Pierson believes that all of us are artists, born with a box of materials and supplies—words, images, song, dance, food, smells, dreams. Read this book to find out why we should open our box, reach in, and pull out our instruments for creating and curating. Few books provide such a quiver full of creative artistry as *The Art of Curating Worship.* —**Leonard Sweet, Drew University, George Fox University, sermons.com**

I loved this book! It offers an evocative framework for deepening the Church's worship experience whether one's worship context is ultra traditional, avant-garde or somewhere in between. Mark Pierson's style is instructive without being pedantic, directive without being prescriptive, practical without being formulaic, and engaging without being provocative. He draws deeply on the wealth of personal experiences he brings to the task as well as the vast theological resources across the Christian tradition. His love for the church and the culture in which it is called resounds clearly throughout its pages. My hope is that this book will inspire a company of worship curators who will continue to explore the rich practices only beginning to take shape here. —**Dr. David Williams, President, Taylor Seminary, Edmonton Alberta.**

I highly recommend Mark Pierson's book *The Art of Curating Worship* to every church leader. It's an inspiring encouragement on why and how worship can be transformed in your community as well as a delicious foretaste into the future or worship. Mark has given us wise advice over the past decade in putting together our multi-media worship installations. This new book will enhance that knowledge.—**Andrew Jones, TallSkinnyKiwi.com**

I am in awe of Mark Pierson's capacity to raise the bar in terms of what we expect from worship, while simultaneously giving us the courage, vision and resources to reach it. This book is a rich and beautiful invitation into all the possibilities that worship offers—and best of all, it just makes you want to put down the book and join his journey. —**Cheryl Lawrie, Director of Spirituality, culture and Context in the Uniting Church in Australia**

With a foreword by Dan Kimball

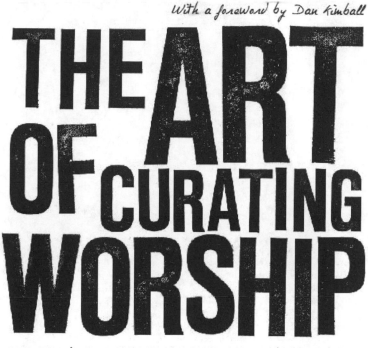

THE ART OF CURATING WORSHIP

RESHAPING THE ROLE OF WORSHIP LEADER

Mark Pierson

sparkhouse press — Minneapolis, MN

THE ART OF CURATING WORSHIP
Reshaping the Role of Worship Leader

Scripture taken from The Message. Copyright © 1993, 1994, 1995, 1996, 2000, 2001, 2002. Used by permission of NavPress Publishing Group.

Cover design: Sharp Seven Design
Book design: Ivy May Weimer

Library of Congress Cataloging-in-Publication Data

Pierson, Mark (Mark Francis)
The art of curating worship : reshaping the role of worship leader / Mark Pierson ; with a foreword from Dan Kimball.
    p. cm.
Includes bibliographical references [and index].
ISBN 978-1-4514-0084-7 (alk. paper)
1. Public worship. I. Title.
BV15.P545 2010
264—dc22   2010025754

The paper used in this publication meets the minimum requirements of American National Standard for Information Sciences — Permanence of Paper for Printed Library Materials, ANSI Z329.48-1984.

Manufactured in the U.S.A.

14 13 12 11   2 3 4 5 6 7 8 9 10

Thanks to Alison Squires, Brenda Rockell, and Stuart McGregor for their musings.

To my grandchildren Taite, Byron, Matthew, and Kate. May this book inspire communities of Christian faith that you and your friends can grow to follow Jesus in.

Contents

Foreword

I t is an incredible honor to be writing a foreword for this book by Mark Pierson. Way back in the early days of what became known as the "emerging church" (before the term got so confusing with so many different meanings), Mark was a leader I followed and paid attention to. I read everything he wrote, found out as much as I could about his church, and was constantly inspired by his passion for the local church, mission, and worship. So many church leaders here in the U.S. don't understand that the roots of much of our alternative worship stem from England, Ireland, New Zealand, and Australia. Those church leaders faced many of the same issues of culture and mission and context that we have found here in the United States, but they did so at least a decade earlier. They were true pioneers for the church. Mark Pierson was among the first to consider what it meant to be a missional church in a changing culture.

What I love about Mark—and what you will discover in this book—is that he loves the local church. He's not interested in big schemes and movements unless they directly relate to the life of a community of faith. Jesus birthed the church as a worshiping community, not simply a group of people who like to do alternative worship for the sake of creative expression. That's Mark's passion—helping people of faith worship in the context of a local community of Jesus-followers on mission together.

This truly isn't a book that's trying to make church relevant, hip, or artistic. Mark begins by asking theological questions: "What is church?" "What is worship?" Without a theological framework, it is far too easy for those interested in alternative worship to put more focus on the creativity of worship than the person of Jesus. We can subtly focus more on worship ideas than theological groundwork. Sounds crazy, but it can happen. Mark truly begins at the core of thinking theologically about worship and the church. I cannot overstate how important that is today and this book does not stray from that.

By encouraging us to stay grounded theologically, Mark allows us to discover something beautiful: freedom. Freedom to create. Freedom to breathe. Freedom to create expressions of worship to God from our hearts and souls that might not fit within the usual boxes of worship we have practiced for so long. Mark teaches us to breathe out our worship to God in truth.

A few years ago I went spelunking. I was underground for hours. Finally we came up out of the cave and as we arose the air was so incredibly fresh and wondrous. It was marvelous to breathe it in. The odd part was that we had gotten used to the air in the cave. After a while it just felt like normal air. It wasn't until we got to the surface and breathed in that fresh air that I realized how stagnant the air was in the cave. In the same way, when we breathe prayer and worship in and out in the same ways we've done for decades, we don't even notice when the air becomes stagnant. We are breathing, but the air isn't as fresh and full as it could be. Mark challenges churches to consider the air we breathe in worship. It's time for us to come out of the cave and breathe in fresh ideas that will lead us to breathe out fresh worship from our hearts, minds, and souls. That doesn't mean straying from truth or chasing after trends or gimmicks or bashing the old or talking about the need for relevance. This book isn't about that. It is about the opening of our hearts and minds to fully breathe our love and passion for God in ways that make sense to our existence as followers of Jesus today.

I imagine there will be many readers who, like me, find themselves consistently in agreement with Mark's vision for worship. They will feel like they have found a kindred heart and aren't alone in how they think of expressing worship. Even though Mark is literally across the globe, I feel as though we have shared hearts and minds around this. When I've wondered if I was crazy for thinking about worship in ways that feel so different from what I've known, I find great encouragement in the ideas Mark writes about here. And it's thrilling to think about how many church leaders will share that feeling and push themselves past their fears and into the possibilities of renewed worship.

I love this book because it is based on the life of the local church. I love this book because it is theology and practice joined together. I love this book because it isn't a "how-to" book as much as it is a sharing of worship-like experiences between friends. I thank Mark for once again guiding us, inspiring us, and leading us in the worship of our Savior and King.

—Dan Kimball, www.dankimball.com

Where I'm Coming From

There is very little truth in this book. There are certainly no absolutes. There are also no lies (that I'm aware of). Like all writing, this book represents the opinions of the writer. It is based on my perspectives, my opinions, and my responses to the situations I have encountered and the path I have stumbled along. It reflects how I see life, faith, and the church. My vision has been shaped by interactions with people who have generously inspired, encouraged, forgiven, and criticized me, but I take responsibility for what I have to say in this book.

I am writing primarily to those who can make a difference to the corporate worship that is rolled out in churches each week. I am also writing to those who have a nagging feeling that all isn't quite right with the current diet, to those who want to see worship engage people outside *and* inside of the church walls and church life. I write from my experience as a participant in the Baptist family of churches in New Zealand and Australia, but also from short-term experiences with churches and leaders of various stripes in Australia, the United Kingdom, Canada, and the United States.

I have been described as a depressed, melancholic cynic. There was a time when I wore that badge proudly. My response to my Pentecostal friends who wanted to cast out my "spirit of cynicism" was that if they did so I would lose my gift to the church. Cynicism isn't always bad. It was—and to a large extent still is—the lens through which I view the life of the church, in general, and the churches of which I have been a part, in particular.

If I had to describe myself now I would probably use the words *concerned* and *grieving*. I'm concerned that it is so difficult to find communal worship that connects me with God. I'm concerned that I meet so many people—of all ages but particularly thirty plus—who consider themselves followers of Christ but can't cope with church and find no nurture or sustenance in its institutions. I'm concerned that too few church leaders and so-called worship leaders have more than a single, narrow model for what they do in public, corporate worship. I'm concerned that they seem unaware they are boring their communities to death with shallow, bland worship. I'm concerned that many of these people have spent several years in theological training institutions that haven't prepared them for the realities of worship and spiritual formation with a congregation. I'm concerned that my young grandsons won't be able to find communities that will nurture their faith without them having to undergo cultural circumcision. All this grieves me greatly.

Yet I've also glimpsed new possibilities and been encouraged and inspired by those glimpses. I don't believe the church as we know it needs to be thrown out. I don't think it needs a new start. I'm not even suggesting that what you're doing in worship should be discarded and replaced. Rather I hope you will be inspired to make the worship you are designing and delivering week by week, in whatever genre, even stronger and more effective in helping people engage with God.

This is a hopeful book, filled with possibilities and ideas that will stimulate your creativity, broaden your horizons, and enlarge your gallery of connections and resources. It is meant to make you think, and reconsider, and imagine. I will talk about what I've seen, what I've tried, and what I've learned. But I tell you all of that not so that you will do what I've done, but so that you can see, and try, and learn as well. In that spirit, this book is descriptive rather than prescriptive. I divide worship into three categories, but that doesn't mean there are only three categories. That's just how I have made the division to suit myself—you might prefer two, or ten. I hope you find yourself disagreeing with me from time to time. I hope you question and challenge what I say.

Mostly, I hope you will contextualize what I say. Your settings for worship will be different from mine. Apart from the basic principles and ideas, very little of what I say will transfer straight across our differing contexts. If there is one single change in approach I believe can transform Christian worship in the West, it is that each community of faith do the work of reframing and contextualizing rather than just copying what has worked somewhere else.

I love the local church and have worked within its leadership structures for more than thirty years. It is my hope that this book will contribute to a discussion that provides the church with a greater awareness of what goes on in public worship. In particular, I hope it will change the way the church engages with artists and the arts, and with culture. I want to see a reformation of the church that leads its community of Jesus-followers to engage with God, with other people, and with the path of justice in the world. I believe that the key to this change is to begin seeing worship as an art form and understanding ourselves as its curators.

Welcome to the journey. I'm delighted to be able to walk with you.

1

Why Change?

> When they said, "Let's go to the house of God," my
> heart leaped for joy. (Ps. 122:1, *The Message*).

I recently talked with a young woman who said she would often go home from church on Sundays and lie on her bed and cry because it depressed her so much. She went because she felt it was what a Christian should do, but it didn't bring her any joy. Increasingly in the West, the kind of joy described in Psalm 122 is nonexistent, even among those who say they are followers of Jesus. I don't think that's what the psalmist, or Jesus, had in mind for us.

Perhaps Psalm 22 better describes our church experiences: "God, God ... my God! Why did you dump me miles from nowhere? Doubled up with pain, I call to God all the day long. No answer. Nothing. I keep at it all night, tossing and turning. And you! Are you indifferent, above it all, leaning back on the cushions of Israel's praise? We know you were there for our parents: they cried for your help and you gave it; they trusted and lived a good life" (Ps. 22:1-5, *The Message*).

I could quote statistics about the decline in church attendance in every country in the West, or decry the blandness of much of what is offered as public worship. But I'd rather give you a brief outline of the journey I have been on and raise the issue I want to focus on for much of this book—the need to understand worship as an art form.

I am, by vocation and experience, a local church pastor. I was raised in a non-church-attending family, which gave me a particular perspective on church life when I began stumbling along as a follower of Jesus at the age of nineteen. I needed to find ways of connecting my newfound faith with what was happening in my life and the lives of my friends. I assumed nothing and questioned everything. That perspective has fed a deep passion for connecting the life of the local church community—and its worship and mission life—with contemporary culture. Or more particularly, with the people who live and move and have their being in the contemporary cultures that form and are forming in our societies.

After a dozen years of being trained and shaped as a pastoral leader by three different, and very generous and tolerant congregations in New Zealand, I found myself wondering why anyone would want to regularly attend a public worship event. It wasn't that there was anything wrong or bad about the events I was part of—in fact some offered profound engagements with God. It was just that, more often than not, I found myself more interested in hanging out with the parents and children in the preschool than wanting to be in a pew.

Then I had an experience that changed my life.

I attended a high-school reunion. Unlike these affairs in the United States our reunions happen only occasionally and usually in honor of an anniversary of the school rather than a particular class. This was the first reunion I had attended in the twenty years since I'd finished school. I was delighted to find a good number of my previous classmates taking the opportunity to see each other.

I'm an introvert, so initially I sat back and observed and listened to the stories being told. I was intrigued that many of the conversations centered on spirituality and faith, and that I was continuously drawn into the conversations. I couldn't believe what I was hearing. Many of my old friends were on spiritual journeys—seeking to find answers that would bring meaning to the experiences and questions of their lives. It wasn't that they were unaware of the spiritual realm—some had experienced vivid and powerful demonstrations of the supernatural. What surprised me was that none of them had found what they were looking for in any church or Christian community. Georgina was involved in the occult; Karen had found her answers in crystals and other New Age options. Most had not even thought to look to the church for what they were seeking, and those who had done so had not found the experience helpful.

The killer blow for me was the realization that if they had come to the church I was leading at the time, they would not have found their answers either. In fact, their questions would have been foreign to and not understood by most of the people in my community.

My school friends all wanted the same things from life I did. They were ordinary New Zealanders wanting satisfying relationships, drug-free children who would make a positive contribution to society, fulfilling life partnerships, stable and satisfying work. We all had similar hopes and dreams and questions, yet I wouldn't want them to come to my church because I knew it would put them off instead of turning them on to Jesus.

Tears filled my eyes as I drove home from the reunion. I determined I would find some way to build a community of faith where people like my former classmates could find a safe and supportive environment in which they could find the spiritual reality they were looking for—the reality I knew existed in following Jesus Christ.

Several years later when the opportunity came to work with a very small and still-shrinking Baptist church in downtown Auckland, I took it. I had no idea what to do. I just knew I wanted a place to belong where the worship and the people enabled me to engage with God without having to step out of the culture I was part of or having to put aside the movies, music, ideas, and conversations that interested me. I figured that a small—and probably dying—church was a good place to start. Change was possible.

RESTORING ART IN WORSHIP

I had no artistic ability and had not been raised in a home that engaged with the arts in any way. (My father did play the mouth organ!) We didn't attend church regularly. I knew almost nothing about the arts when I began pastoring, but by this stage I sensed that the arts and worship needed to get back in bed with each other as they had in earlier centuries. My initial motivation to engage with the arts was to find vehicles for expression by the small but increasing number of artists and other creatives of all hues who were gathering at that small church, now called Cityside Baptist Church, where I was pastoral leader in the late 1990s.

Late at night on September 14, 1997, I wrote in my journal:

> I'm beginning to understand worship and worship preparation much more as an art form than an organizational task. To see myself as a producer/ preparer of worship for myself and others, as a worship curator—someone who takes the pieces provided and puts them in a particular setting and makes a particular arrangement of them, considering juxtaposition, style, light, shade, etc. A maker of

context rather than a presenter of content. A provider of a frame inside of which the elements are arranged and rearranged to convey a particular message to the worshiper. This message may or may not be obvious, may or may not be similar to the message conveyed to/perceived by another worshiper.

Worship is art. Art can be worship.
I provide worship experiences for others to participate in.
I am an artist
    a framer
    a curator
    a recontexter

I have experience; I learn, I train, I improve my skills,
I reflect, I worship, I participate, I risk, I trust. . . .

The next decade saw many more creative people join and participate in our community, most with sad stories of how their craft had been ignored or abused or misunderstood by church communities or individuals. They found trust, openness, and acceptance at Cityside, as well as encouragement to participate and use their skills in worship and mission without necessarily having to include anything that was overtly Christian.

At that same time, I was on a very steep learning curve, soaking up all I could about the creative process and how artists worked, trying to figure out how we could provide sanctuary for them and still maintain a specifically Christian context for them and their work. They were, and continue to be, my teachers.

The projects we entered into were not without their critics—usually people outside our community and who were ignorant of the objects they were criticizing—yet we were seeing real transformation in the lives of our artists and those who participated as viewers or in some other way. Running an art exhibition, a new media night, or an electronic music concert in themselves held little appeal for me as a pastoral leader. It was the formative power of art and its processes that I wanted to capture. While I always wanted what we did as a church community to sustain a *Christian* faith and spirituality, I also wanted spiritual depth and real connection with the emotions and realities of the stories of people, Christian or not.

I wanted what we did to have integrity. I didn't want art as a hook to draw people in, so we could then hit them with something else. Nor did I want kitschy art that reproduced biblical panoramas or Sunday-school-like works, regardless of how "realistic" they might be. My experience in churches had been that a painting about the crucifixion needed to contain three crosses on a hill with men nailed to them. The feeling was that nothing worthwhile (read *of value* or *Christian*) could be conveyed in any other way. But I had become convinced—again intuitively—that the more interpreted and translated a work was, the better it would connect with people who had never considered the Christian faith worth investigating. I felt strongly that there was a need for us to put some mystery back into the Christian story.

Quite quickly, it became obvious from comments made verbally and in writing that people who participated in producing and consuming some of the projects we put together were encountering God in some unexpected but significant and—to me—very rewarding ways. The question was, how and why this was happening? Was it random? Was it valid? Was it really God? I wondered how the experience of God differed depending on a person's experience or knowledge of the Christian faith. I worried it might be dangerous to sometimes present work with so little overtly Christian content—was allowing such a broad range of interpretations encouraging heresy? I questioned whether this stuff was even helpful in the journey of Christian spiritual formation or if it was merely froth and bubble as our critics said it was.

Maybe the arts were just supporters of the real message that would come later in verbal form? Or could electronic music, video loops, and painting be beautiful and personally uplifting, *and* be appropriate vehicles for substantive theology and personal transformation?

All of this wondering led me to dig into everything I could find that talked about using art in spiritual formation. It turned out much had been written about how to use art in churches—especially about the dangers of doing so. I could find almost nothing that explored why such approaches might be of value or what was happening in these encounters between people and art. The arts were referred to only in relation to their helpfulness in accessing the culture, never for spiritual formation or worship itself. Many writers reflected deeply on the current and future shape of the church and its worship (among other issues) but made no significant reference to art in spiritual formation or as a medium for engaging God. In other words, at Cityside we were making it up as we went along.

The creative-worship projects at Cityside Church made it one of the first communities in the alternative-worship movement,[1] the forerunner to the emerging-church movement. Very little formal writing arose from and about the largely British-based alternative-worship movement—that which did was mostly of a practical nature, telling the stories of various alternative communities as a way of encouraging others to do likewise. In contrast, when things alternative hit the United States some years later, the printing presses could barely run fast enough to keep up with the volumes being written. From what I have read, these books often make worthwhile contributions to our understanding of the changing church context in which worship and mission take place. They describe what those activities could look like in particular contexts. They also encourage the use of arts in worship. Yet none that I have found go beyond an explanation and description of essentially pragmatic practices. I have been able to find very little literature investigating or reflecting on how people respond in worship and what they respond to, and, therefore, how a worship event might be crafted or designed. We lack any developed theoretical framework to guide our worship design so we just repeat what we have always done, but louder or with more projectors or candles.

Nor have I been able to find any significant discussion of art *as* worship, or what it is about art that worshipers respond to, or how the arts shape worship or the faith journey of a community at worship. Timothy L. Carson has a very helpful chapter, "Betwixt and Between: Worship and Liminal Reality," in his excellent book, *Transforming Worship*[2], but the chapter is less than four pages long. Len Sweet has provided us with his useful EPIC approach to worship—Experiential, Participatory, Image-Driven, and Communal—which he develops in numerous writings.[3] Sweet states that the changing contemporary culture demands mainline Protestant worship move from providing rational responses to experiential ones, from a few representatives leading the congregation to broader participation, from being word-based to being image-driven, from isolated individualism to worship that promotes community. He clearly understands the milieu in which the church is currently operating and offers insightful perspectives on how the church needs to respond to and participate in that environment. But he doesn't set out to help someone wanting to know how to grapple with an understanding of art and worship for next Sunday morning at 11 a.m. The intersection of art, worship, and pastoral ministry appears to be a rarely considered topic.

ABUSING THE ARTS

What is generally advocated in the resources I have seen is the kind of approach I found in the vision statement of a Melbourne church: "We will use the arts more," or, as one recent writer advocates,

"We must rely more than ever on art, music, literature, and drama to communicate our message." This reflects an attitude that I find abusive of the arts and creativity. It sees them as little more than tools for evangelism and persuasion, and fails to appreciate the intrinsic value of the creative process. To limit the arts in this way generally results in the view that the work must include the name of Jesus or an image of the cross along with substantial text so that "the message" is stated without possibility of misinterpretation. Any sense of beauty, spirituality, creativity, deep engagement, mystery, the active presence of the Holy Spirit in a medium or work, or the idea that God could be encountered in a work is ignored or, worse still, denied.

Consider this critique of the abusive attitude on display at one megachurch that was using drama as its art form:

> Drama is used to set up a pedagogic moment, servant to the pastor's message; it is not intended to function pedagogically on its own, nor is it intended in any way to function in a sacramental mode. Drama is not considered a suitable way to preach the gospel when the goal is to raise a question and provide an answer that gives clear assurance and a "how-to" application; the drama sets up the problem, the message offers the solution.[4]

This is in stark contrast to the experience described by Mike Riddell on viewing *Black Phoenix*—an art installation using the full-size prow of a fishing boat ravaged by fire—by New Zealand artist Ralph Hotere:

> This was resurrection broken out of verbal confines, bludgeoning the imagination and challenging any resistance. No sermon I have ever heard has

approached the power or lingering effect of that artwork. Here was no abstract discussion of rumours of immortality; this was immediate, visceral and inescapable. I was broken open by it, and left overwhelmed and exhausted. It was a religious experience, in the deepest sense of the term. How was it, I pondered later, that I had been moved at this level by an encounter entirely devoid of specific content? Why should the burnt-out hulk of a fishing vessel evoke such deep meditations on mortality?[5]

I believe art is capable of far more than communicating a message: it is capable of conveying the voice of God and harboring an encounter with God. In the West, we are in the midst of a massive upsurge in interest in "using" the creative arts in worship and mission. We need to undergird that interest with an understanding of what happens in the engagement with art, and reflection on the implications of that engagement for pastoral ministry and spiritual formation. Without this analysis, we are in danger of repeating the short-term and shallow responses of the past that relied heavily, if not entirely, on pragmatism. It's time the church understood designing worship as an art, rather than a project, and especially not as a project that uses art. This perspective calls for a new way of thinking and talking about worship.

A VOCABULARY OF WORSHIP

There is no "one size fits all" when it comes to worship. Every person should be able to experience transformative engagement with God without having to adopt a new culture or persona. Encouraging this engagement is the role of the church, and it can take many forms. It is certainly not limited to a particular style of worship. So I am not proposing any one style, or even a raft of styles. I am proposing a new way of looking at the worship we design or lead, regardless of whether it is charismatic, evangelical, contemporary, liturgical, Pentecostal, high church, low church, or no church. I had two church experiences recently that will show you why I see the need for new ways of thinking and talking about what we do corporate worship.

I had heard a lot about a relatively new community that met in a warehouse space in the suburbs. They apparently do a lot with artists and the arts, so I was interested in checking them out. An up-to-date website gave me times, place, directions, so I set out to join them for morning worship. Signage at the main road and further down the side road directed me easily to the warehouse behind a shopping mall and sports grounds.

Then my discomfort began. Which door of three should I go through? There was no one at the doors to greet me or point me in the right direction. I followed several deaf mutes (or so I concluded as they never acknowledged my presence) into the building and sat at one of many small round café tables with four to six chairs around them. I chose a table with bags and jackets on a couple of the chairs on the assumption that someone was sitting at the table and would soon join me.

Ten minutes went by without anyone speaking to me or acknowledging me. The jacket and bag owners stealthily collected their gear and sat at another table. Sitting alone, I smiled across the room at a young baby draped over her mother's shoulder. The space was cold, and the bare concrete floor chilled my feet. The unlit gas heaters stood as sentries—guarding against warmth perhaps? The worship leader was pleasant to look at, and I couldn't stop looking at her because she never looked at me. In fact, she never looked at anyone—she had her eyes closed (in worship?) the entire time she was "leading" us. She only opened them to check the next song. The blind leading the blind.

I loved seeing young children wander freely from person to person, cared for by the community. I was delighted that two young people with intellectual disabilities seemed to be accepted and integrated into this community at worship. But my delight turned to anger as the service progressed, and these people became the brunt of laughter as they were allowed to wander around the stage and interrupt the song leader and preacher. They were used as light entertainment. I am a parent to an intellectually disabled son and feel this is nasty stuff. The sermon was long, rambling, and unengaging. I left having spoken only to the parents of the baby I'd smiled at. I was desperate to get to the heater in my car and defrost my feet.

That evening I made my way to a one-hundred-year-old Anglican church. It was easy to find my way inside, even in the dark and with no one at the door, as this old stone building was built and positioned to be welcoming. Central heating took the chill off nicely. It was an ambient, open-ended, fully curated, nonsinging, reflective service (by the end of this book you will be familiar with all those terms). The otherwise dark worship space was lit by thirty candles. Music was a free-form jazz/ambient mix of electronica, sax, trumpet, guitar, upright bass, drums, and percussion. The musicians played from the rear of the sanctuary, and, from time to time, I would turn in my pew to see them—the sound was more important than the sound makers. A small icon and incense bowl occupied the center of the space while a looped image of water flowing over rocks was projected on a screen behind the incense. A handout of thoughtful questions provided stimulus for my postsermon reflections. I left having met with God.

I ended the day wondering why anyone would attend a service like the one I'd gone to that morning. Why do we put the musicians on a raised platform at the front? Why do we insist on sitting participants at café tables? Why do we talk as if people are important and then act as if they aren't? Why do we assume that "if we build it they will come" and keep on coming, regardless of how badly we treat them?

I have often been aligned with the emerging church. That doesn't bother me—there are many great people in the same alignment—but I don't like the term much. I prefer to think and talk about what I do as being part of the "reemerging church." It seems to me that the former implies something new that will come in over the top of the old and push it aside, that new is better than old. Café tables trump pews. Musicians at the front trump the organ console at the back. *Reemerging* speaks to me of building on what has gone before, of discovering new ways of connecting with a changed and changing culture, and of using what we have learned from the past to become part of the future. It allows room for new missional attitudes to come from inside or outside of the inherited church, all seeking and needing new forms of worship.

Another way of looking at it is to say that the vocabulary is still much the same, but a new language needs to be made out of that vocabulary. So I'm not proposing that we ditch preaching, or singing, or prayers, or any other element of our current worship patterns. I'd like to give those terms some new content, suggest some different perspectives on them, and explore various new ways we could combine them in order to have people engage with God more deeply. I'd also like to look beneath the surface of the worship we design and see if we can find a way of talking about it that is transferable across styles and that expands our understanding of what, and where, and how worship might happen.

That's what this book is about.

2

First Things First

Before I get started on a new language for worship, I'd like to back up a bit and ask some questions that I consider vital. All of them need to be answered before you can determine what worship should look like for your community.

The most visible roots of the alternative-worship movement go back to the Nine O'clock Service in the United Kingdom in the late 1980s. I was delighted when alternative worship eventually became alternative *church* and, still later, emerging church. We had finally acknowledged that the future of the church didn't lie in small groups of disenfranchised postchurchers navel-gazing to house music by candlelight. Despite their shortcomings, the new terms recognized that the future lay in something broader than worship alone.

My concern now is that the emerging-church movement isn't asking deep enough questions about its practice. It often seems to be doing worship badly, having settled for froth and bubble—for technology and couches and cafés instead of true change. Much of what I read and have experienced suggests that a church or worship event that purports to be "new and exciting" is, in many cases, just the "old and unengaging" placed in a new setting. We know what we don't want, but we don't know how to create anything truly appropriate for our new setting. In many places, alternative worship has been embraced by the mother church, and she can give the appearance of having been changed by her returning prodigal. Much positive change has happened both in inherited churches and emerging and alternative gatherings—though neither the alternative nor emerging labels are broad enough to include all that is happening in communities of faith around the world. Despite unleashing all that stunning creativity, in the pews on a Sunday it's mostly business as usual.

Andrew Jones, who blogs at http://tallskinnykiwi.typepad.com, describes ten categories of emerging churches that he sees operating around the developed world.[6] The list includes categories that were considered to be outside the bounds of Christianity just a decade ago but that are now mostly accepted:

1. Culture-based communities such as skater and goth churches
2. Gen X, Postmodern, and Emergent churches
3. New-monastic orders and intentional communities
4. House churches
5. Cyberchurch and online communities
6. Alternative worship and fresh expression churches
7. Pub and coffee shop churches
8. Contemplative prayer movement
9. Churchless Christians
10. Social-enterprise-based communities

This list of mostly missional enterprises is exciting and encouraging. I wonder how each group will do worship and how much that worship will be shaped to best reflect the culture of its community. Will most groups simply assume that the models they have from other settings can be imposed on a new setting? What begins as a search for alternative ways of worshiping with integrity easily settles on a single worship style that looks a lot like what it was protesting against. My experience of these new missional enterprises isn't wide enough to make a definitive statement, but, sadly, I haven't seen much that suggests they are developing new practices indigenous to their communities. Does this reflect a lack of examples to follow or a lack of questioning what has gone before?

ASKING BETTER QUESTIONS

The answer to the church's problems with worship doesn't lie in greater creativity, or better music, or more relevance, or a better understanding of culture or even of the arts. The solution lies in asking better questions. Or at least that's where it starts. If we don't ask the right questions, we can fall for the "Ashram Cat" fallacy.

The Ashram Cat

When the guru sat down to worship each evening, the ashram cat would get in the way and distract the worshipers. So he ordered the cat be tied up during evening worship. Long after the guru died, the cat continued to be tied up during evening worship. And when the cat eventually died, another cat was brought to the ashram so that it could be dutifully tied up during evening worship. Centuries later, learned treatises were written by the guru's disciples on the essential role of a cat in all properly conducted worship.

That's often the way we operate in the church. We don't ask the right questions, and we overlay our past experiences—or reactions against them—on what we think we should do for the future. I worked with a mission group that provided a lunch meal to marginalized and homeless people. Some staff members were adamant that we should not close on public holidays. This caused tension with the staff who wanted those days off. We were only open Monday through Thursday, but most public holidays fell on a Monday. Changing our days to Tuesday through Friday would largely solve the problem. But we had always been open Monday through Thursday, hadn't we? When the question was asked and some research done, we discovered that years ago we had, in fact, been open Tuesday through Friday, but the days had been altered to accommodate a worker who had university classes on Fridays! There was no good reason why we could not change again.

You will find similar stories around why Sunday evening services tend to be more evangelistic than morning ones, why Baptist churches use "thimbles" and diced bread for communion, why we sit in rows, why we have twenty minutes of singing, and why we have many more elements considered essential in all "properly conducted" worship. Asking the right questions is vital if we are to understand what is important to retain and what can be changed. I suggest starting with two:

1. What is church?
2. What is worship?

What Is Church?

Why do we come together as Christians at all? What do we come together to do that's so important? In other words, for what does the church exist? What is the purpose of a church? Large tomes have been written in answer to that question. As a practicing pastor, I have a very simple working definition that I keep before me: *the reason we come together as a church community is to sustain people in their following of Jesus Christ in the world.*

Every word and phrase in that statement is important, and none can be omitted: Sustain. . .people. . .following Jesus. . .in the world. It's the church, not a service club or a hobby group (although it might sustain people who are part of those groups). It exists to sustain the particular people who are part of its community, in their following of Christ, in the worlds they are part of. I think mission and evangelism are inherent in following Jesus, but sometimes people want to make it more explicit. For them I add, *and to introduce others to that journey.*

When I need to make decisions about our church community and where I should direct my time and energy, that definition keeps me focused. It helps me to decide what our core business is and whether or not we should pick up a new idea when it comes along. It also helps define what we do in worship.

What Is Worship?

The heart of the life of any Christian community is worship. No matter what form the church takes, its life will always involve worship of some kind, generally corporate worship. By *worship* I don't mean just the singing part of a service, or any other single element of the gathering. I am not talking about private, individual worship. I am referring to any corporate event that encourages people to engage with God. Rather than referring to this as a worship service, I prefer to use the term *worship event.* I will use this phrase to encompass the whole event that is called "worship" or "church," regardless of its setting.

Worship tastes vary widely from person to person. One person's meaningful liturgy is another's boring tradition. The stimulating charismatic choruses loved by many are merely soulless repetition to others. But personal taste is no excuse for poorly presented worship or for worship that doesn't engage people, whatever style it might pursue.

If we assume corporate worship is something worth doing in that it helps to sustain us in our following of Jesus in the world (and I would always make that assumption), we must ask ourselves what worship is. My working definition is again very simple: *Worship is a person or persons responding to the Trinitarian community of God, with heart, soul, mind, and strength* (or as Eugene Peterson translates those words from Luke 10:27 in *The Message*, with "passion, prayer, intelligence, and muscle").

This is the definition I keep in mind when I am putting together a worship event. As a pastor, I'm trying to help people encounter God and respond to that encounter in meaningful and transforming ways. Worship is both about God and about us. I don't readily take to definitions that suggest worship is all about God. Does God need our worship? Is God the ultimate ego? I don't think so. But I know that I need to worship God. I like the definition of worship I heard Donna Dinsmore give: "itsallaboutgoditsallaboutus."[7]

If you are having trouble clarifying what worship is or should be about for your community, you may find theologian Susan White's approach helpful. She says we need to ask the question, "If I had never been to a worship service before, what would I think was going on? What would I know about the purpose of the gathering, of this community, and about the God to be met here from being present in this service of Christian worship?"[8]

As you lead your community in worship old or new, you need to come up with your own working definitions of *church* and *worship*, definitions that reflect the values and traditions of your community. As you do, try to avoid quoting biblical texts about either—you want something that describes the outcomes you are aiming for. These outcomes will reflect biblical values, but answering these questions in your own words helps them become something you will own, use, and refer back to.

Answering these questions could be a group effort. Or the process might start with you offering some definitions and getting feedback from a few people you trust. It might be that you are the one charged with coming up with these answers. No matter who is involved in the process, remember that you are not aiming for a comprehensive definition. You are looking for something memorable that can guide your decision making as you design and deliver a worship event or the elements within an event. Donna Dinsmore's definition doesn't work as a guiding statement, but it offers a particular perspective on worship. Your working definition will need to be more concrete and measurable. Each year at Cityside, our annual report consists of people answering the question, "How has being at Cityside this past year helped sustain you in your following of Jesus in your world?"

Once you come up with simple working definitions of *church* and *worship*, there are some other questions to ask. And even if you already know what your definitions will be, these issues need to be given an airing.

People

Who is in my community? Knowing who is in your community of faith will add depth and breadth to your mission and ministry. Even though I have my working definitions of *church* and *worship*, before I will plan a worship event, I need to ask, "What is the best way to sustain *these* people in their following of Jesus Christ in the world?" Not the people I hope to attract but *this* group? To plan these activities with anyone in mind other than the community that gathers is the fastest way I know for worship to stay shallow and narrow. It is also the quickest route to a lack of integrity that will be picked up by newcomers.

Theology

What do we understand the gospel to be about? What is our Christology? What is the role of the Holy Spirit, and how do people become followers of Jesus? How will our worship reflect and renew our beliefs? And so on.

Missiology

When I think through the theology of my community, I have to ask where that theology takes us. What arises from our Christology? How does it inform our way of being church? What values will drive us? What will our worship say about what we believe about the world, justice, the environment, our mission?

Ecclesiology

How will we do church? This is very different from our previously discussed questions: What is worship? What is church? It involves broader questions like: What sacraments will we celebrate? Will children be involved? Who will or won't lead us? How will our leaders be chosen?

When it comes time to plan a worship event, it's essential that I have the answers to these questions because they influence how I will shape that worship. And yet I have to begin the planning process with a metaphorical blank page, with no assumptions made. It's just me (or my team), reflecting on the answers and creating something that will be meaningful to my community in light of those answers. None of this happens in a vacuum, of course. I have to draw on the best of Christian tradition and history, all of my combined experience and skills, my understanding of theology and of culture, and all the courage I can muster.

This is not necessarily a solo pursuit, but it might be. In an existing community with well-established patterns of life, any new thinking may be a luxury not afforded you. In that case, thinking through these questions in a group gives you momentum and a shared story and journey that will help ease the way as you introduce new ideas into your worship events.

CREATING WORSHIP

Finally, we can get to the questions we most often misguidedly begin with: How will we design and deliver our worship events? What will corporate worship—worship that will be sustaining for this group of people—look like for us? And can we ask these questions without looking for a quick fix solution to a problem in our worship?

Having come this far, when we finally get to ask those questions, I believe anything goes.

Anything goes.

Of course there are some lessons learned over the last two thousand years of church history that you'd be foolish to ignore. And anything that reflects more of your ego and thirst for power than a desire toward sustaining the community in their following of Christ in the world, well, that's out too.

As a trained, educated, and self-aware pastoral leader, you know the people you are among, and you have some ideas about what will be helpful and what won't. You know what will offend rather than transform. You understand Jesus' command was to "feed my sheep" and not "herd and drive my sheep." You are aware of the learning styles, pastoral needs, and past experiences of your community. You understand the stages of spiritual formation they are at. So your ideas on what will sustain them and what will enable them to engage with God automatically set parameters for what you will do with them.

It's within those parameters that anything goes. I'm not just saying that for effect. I mean it. If we work from a place of wide-open possibility, then we are far less likely to fall into patterns of simply repeating what we've done before or, worse yet, copying someone else's worship style.

In the 1987 movie *When Harry Met Sally*, the main characters, Harry and Sally, eat at a restaurant and discuss the reasons they will never date. During the discussion Sally fakes an orgasm in order to convince Harry that it can be done convincingly. By the end of her prolonged exhibition, the whole restaurant is watching and listening. The scene ends by cutting to a middle-aged female patron at another table who looks at the waitress, gestures toward Sally, and says, "I'll have what she's having."

This classic movie line points to a problem that's rife in churches— we assume that what works for others will work for us. That approach sells our communities short and lacks integrity. It reflects a short-sighted and lazy approach to worship. It isn't good enough for us to just regurgitate what has worked somewhere else. Good worship takes much more hard work and insight than that.

Using a process like the one I've suggested means you are unlikely to import what another church has done without taking great care to ensure that it has been reframed and contextualized to your own community. "I'll have what she's having" just isn't good enough.

Neither is it good enough to carry on with what has always been done in the past without asking where those ideas came from and whether they continue to reflect the needs of your community. People change; faith communities change; cultural expectations change. Maggi Dawn summed this up beautifully when she said, "You have to change to stay the same."[9] Worship can't be meaningful and transformative when it's stagnant.

I am not advocating getting rid of the past or ignoring the many wonderful traditions we have inherited. I'm not suggesting there is one right or best way to do worship nor am I suggesting that the shape of your worship event needs to change. I'm advocating a new way of talking and thinking about what we do in worship, and particularly how we plan and design worship events. Instead of asking, "What songs will we sing on Sunday?" we could ask, "What ways can I get people to engage with this text and encounter God?" or, "What segue will best connect this song with the prayer of confession that follows it?" or, "Is there one really helpful song we need to sing this morning?" These questions will lead to authentic, meaningful worship within our usual pattern, in ways that carrying on the same old thing for unknown reasons never can.

Changing the way we think about worship, while very important, is only a small step in renewing our churches. We also need a new way of talking about how we design corporate worship. We need a new vocabulary with which to build a new language for worship.

3

Curation: The Glue That Holds It All Together

Before I explore a variety of terms old and new that we can use when talking about and designing worship, one single term, *curation*, needs to be unwrapped before that conversation will make sense.

Understanding the role of a worship curator is the key to changing the way we design worship and, therefore, the way we enable people to engage with God in public corporate worship. I first coined the term *worship curator* after having two very different and unconnected experiences. The first was the high-school reunion I mentioned earlier where I was struck by the number of spiritual seekers who either hadn't considered looking to the church for answers or had done so and not found anything helpful. The second occurred a few years later when I visited a quite bizarre art installation titled, *I Had a Thought*. I first described this in the book, *The Prodigal Project*:

> The entrance to the art gallery had become a dressing room. My daughter and I were each fitted with a clear plastic body suit (stapled to fit around our contours), plastic bags were tied over our shoes, surgeon's rubber

gloves put on our hands, and the outfit topped off with a white hardhat with full clear visor. Looking like we were ready for a DIY tour of Chernobyl we were ushered through a décor of hanging plastic strips into a huge white space. Floor of white polythene. Wall and ceiling painted white. Large floor-to-ceiling flexible mirrors along the walls distorted our movements.

A dozen or so big circular children's paddling pools were spread around the space. Each of the pools had a fountain—spurting paint. The pools were each filled with a different coloured paint. Occasionally paint sprayed down at random intervals from shower hoses hidden in the ceiling. The space and audience were splattered in paint! It was confusing—not what I expected in an art gallery—and wonderful; we were part of the installation. Participants, not just spectators.

I have no idea now what the installation was meant to be about. I don't think I did back then! According to the gallery notes it was something about "forcing a confrontation between audience anticipation and participation." All I could think about as we slipped around the paint-splashed floor between the fountains and pools, and stood under paint drips and sprays in our child's-play version of space suits was: "Wouldn't it be great if we could do worship in a setting like this?" Active participation with open-ended interpretation. Room to move physically and cognitively. Creative context and content. Andy Warhol goes to church! If I could find some way of providing this kind of context and setting for theologically sound Christian worship, then maybe I'd have something that my old school friends could relate to. Maybe even a setting in which they could begin to understand something of how the gospel might be good news for them. Another journey of discovery had begun for me.[10]

That journey led me to develop my understanding of the role of worship curator. For some years, I'd been putting together weekly community worship events, theme-specific ambient-worship spaces (at Pentecost and Good Friday for example), and what I would now describe as transitional worship events. These drew heavily on ideas from art installations I had seen and read about, and, while they were interesting, I was also aware that the worship I was designing and experiencing was too often isolated from its surroundings—both physical and cultural—to say nothing of the people it was intended for. I felt there should be more integration and integrity between context and content.

I felt that the context was at least as important as the content, perhaps more so from a communication and engagement perspective. I kept thinking of the old Marshall McLuhan idea of the medium being the message and the more recent "context as content."[11] Picking up the term from art exhibitions, I started talking about myself as a worship curator rather than a worship leader. If I understand worship as "a person or person's responding to the Trinitarian community of God with heart, soul, mind, and strength," then it seems clear to me that this will be something that is curated rather than led.

THE CURATOR

The term *curator* comes from the Latin *curare* meaning "to care for." A British website advertising the job of curator says, "A museum or gallery curator acquires, cares for, develops, displays and interprets a collection of artifacts or works of art in order to inform, educate and entertain the public."[12] Interestingly it is also a legal term for "the guardian of a minor, lunatic, or other incompetent."[13] Perhaps both have some implications for worship curators!

The rise of the curator in an art gallery and museum context is—while not new—newly developed, and definitions abound. Until the early twentieth century, artists showed their work either privately or in collective exhibitions that they organized themselves. The increasing professionalization and specialization of this role gave rise to the curator. Traditionally, the curator was seen as a rather academic presence in a museum, researching, archiving, cataloging, collecting, and restoring artifacts of historical and aesthetic value. Today a curator may do everything from dealing with staff, to running the publicity for an exhibition, to writing explanatory notes for gallery installations. It is somewhere in the midst of that spectrum that I situate the role of a worship curator.

The curator of an art installation is responsible for the selection and design of that installation. Imagine a large room in a gallery. In the center of the room stands a collection of packing crates and boxes. Each has within it a piece of art chosen by the curator or delivered to her as part of a specific exhibition. She will be unpacking the artifacts and placing them around the space. She will be taking into consideration—and maybe even altering them to better suit her purposes—the color of the walls, the size and shape of the space, the height of the ceiling, the lighting levels, the temperature, where people enter and exit, and so on. All these factors will affect where and how the artifacts are placed. Will they go against the walls or out from them? Will people be able to walk around an object or just view it from the front or sides? How high will an object be placed? How close to other objects? What will be included and what omitted? In what order will they be presented and with how much or how little explanation? These and dozens of other factors—many of them intuitive and learned from experience, training, and the expressed desires of the artist—will determine the final look and feel of the exhibition.

THE WORSHIP CURATOR

In a similar way, the worship curator is responsible not just for the singing part of a church service (as the misnamed worship leader usually is), but for the whole event—from the moment people enter the door until they leave and everything in between. A good worship curator unpacks the elements of the service in a particular space she has thought about and deliberately arranged. She is aware of lighting levels, temperature, seating, projections, sound, and every element that contributes to the worship experience. She decides what should be printed on handouts, a data projector, or an overhead projector. She determines how much or how little explanation is needed for people to be able to participate fully in the worship. She guides people through worship and connects the various elements of the service together into a flow, including selecting songs or readings as needed. She understands why the church exists and what worship is about. She knows the church calendar and is engaged with the world outside the church. She is theologically trained, pastorally attuned, and draws on her intuition and experience to facilitate the best possible worship experience for the community that is gathered.

Of course this is the ideal—the big-picture view. The role of the worship curator in any actual worship event varies considerably and depends on the context in which worship is being curated. The role will be different in a liturgical 11 a.m. church setting than it would be in an outdoor sacred-space event. I should also add that while the curator is in overall care of the whole worship event, she is not doing everything. She is coordinating the participation of others.

It is also possible to be curator of a single element of the event—say, the prayers of confession. This limits the scope of the curator but is no less valid as a function. The curator might be the pastor but is just as likely to be a layperson. At the church where I initially developed this concept, we eventually had a group of four curators who rotated through each month. These four people were led by a paid staff person, but they had a great deal of autonomy; whoever was assigned a particular week was responsible for coordinating and holding together the various elements of that worship event.

Curating worship, as opposed to leading worship, allows me to shape a worship event with both internal and external integrity while still being open ended in the ways I think worship should be. This perspective on the art of worship is not about a certain style or format. It's about how the curator works in a particular medium—worship. The principles are transferable across all styles of worship and all cultures.

I'll get into more detail about how all of these pieces play out and come together shortly. But before moving into that practical level, I want to go deeper into the values and ideals behind worship curation. I'll begin with two essential processes a curator needs to go through each and every time she is putting together a worship event: aggregation and pruning.

Aggregation

In a web post about digital music and other media, Mike Shatzkin describes the importance of aggregation in any curated context. He writes, "Aggregation is one of the core concepts of content presentation. . . . [It] simply means pulling together things which are not necessarily connected."[14] Before curation can begin, aggregation must take place. Resources must be collected—ideas, materials, songs, liturgy, music tracks, video clips, slides, images, people, and so on.

Failing to go through the aggregation stage can lead to bland and boring worship that, even if curated in other ways, is mostly a repeated or regurgitated version of the week before. Aggregation is what keeps the worship curator fresh, inspired, creative, and better able to encourage engagement with God despite the broad range of lives, and loves, and hates of the worshiping community. It also takes a lot of time and is easily neglected when under the pressure of time.

Rather than thinking of aggregation as a task, however, I suggest thinking of it as a lifestyle. It involves developing an ability to see the stuff of ordinary life—stuff going on in the culture around your community—and bring it into the worship event in ways that enhance the ability of the worshipers to engage with God with heart, soul, mind, strength. It might involve visiting art galleries (especially installation art), reading architecture and design magazines, talking with artists about their processes, and exposing yourself to as wide a range of aural and visual experiences as possible.

Recently I purchased a work by artist Amanda Watson. She had taken canvases rejected from earlier painting sessions and cut them into two-inch squares. She then impaled thirty or so of these pieces on a nail driven through a piece of timber. The works were called *Dud Stacks*. I saw in this the possibility of the "dud" or failure parts of our lives being impaled on a nail and offered to God as a confession. I used this idea as an interactive worship station on a recent Good Friday.

A friend of mine had a pile of cheap white umbrellas, so I purchased one hundred of them. I later used twenty-four to make a projector screen for an ambient video loop in one of our services. A recently discovered book on simple shelters from countries around the world has me thinking about putting together a worship event around the idea of hospitality and the sacred places in our lives. I'll use the book when the idea finds its right time and place.

Most of us are good at collecting readings, prayers, and songs, and perhaps the odd drama or film clip that we will choose from when setting up next week's order of service. Aggregation goes wider and deeper to include every aspect of the cultures and subcultures that make up the lives of the people who will be worshiping. This takes us back to the "anything goes" statement in the previous chapter. There is nothing that can't be included in the worship curator's aggregation, no matter how disparate items might seem. I keep track of my aggregation by scribbling ideas, quotes, words, and comments in a notebook, and by tossing articles and objects in small boxes. I go through all of these regularly looking for inspiration.

But aggregation is not curation. It's a necessary precursor, but good worship is not simply the result of putting a bunch of interesting elements in the right order. Curating first calls for pruning.

Pruning

Mike Shatzkin illustrates his thesis with a description that is helpful to our understanding of worship. He says, "Newspapers are obviously aggregators and curators. The differences in their curation create their brand. *The New York Times* leaves out the comics. *The New York Post* leaves out the multi-syllable words. *The Daily News* beefs up its sports section and, for years, was known for having the best pictures. But one thing has been common to all of them and to all other newspapers: they all cover the waterfront."[15]

Each newspaper sells its advertising against its brand, the result of its pruned aggregate, i.e., what it keeps in. No newspaper prints everything available to it. So, over time, their aggregation gets narrower. If readers or advertisers, or both, start to not like the way this pruning is being done, they will look for newspapers that better connect with who they are and how they live, or want to live, their lives. Realizing this, the newspaper may broaden its aggregate and change its criteria for pruning in the hope of attracting readers back, or of keeping new readers. If it doesn't, it goes out of business.

I'm sure you can see the ways this concept connects with the church, and, in particular, with worship events. The stakes are more than financial for the worship curator. We are involved in the business of designing worship that will enable people to engage with God in ways that will be transformative for them individually, communally, and ultimately for the world.

The church faces many of the same issues that newspapers do in contemporary culture. Most people buy a newspaper for a few articles or sections, not for everything in it. I rarely read the sports pages and only glance through the automotive section, but I read most articles of local and national news. I always read the business section of my paper but never buy the *Financial Times* because it doesn't have much local or national news in it. You need to determine what your community needs from the worship event you are curating, knowing that not every piece of the worship experience will connect with every person.

That's why every church worship event needs to contain a variety of content born out of the aggregation/pruning process. Ideas might have been discarded because the curator didn't like them, or identify with them, or felt they weren't theologically sound or appropriate to the setting. They might have been considered unrelated to the theme or understanding of worship. Whatever the criteria, people will participate in that worship and that church because they find that some or most (rarely all) of the elements are helpful to them, connect with them, or nurture them spiritually. These elements are the reason—whether stated or unrecognized—individuals stay at a particular church or attend a particular worship event.

If one of the elements changes, say, an academic preacher is replaced by one more likely to quote a movie star than a theologian, then the worshiper for whom the academic-preaching element was especially appreciated will likely decide that God is telling her to move on. She can do this more easily than ever before because in our contemporary world she can get the preaching she wants from a hundred sources, without having to get in her car and travel, sit in a pew, or even get out of her pajamas if she doesn't want to.

That's why the role of a worship curator is more important now than it has ever been. Good curation, based on solid aggregation and careful pruning, enables the worship event to better connect with the realities and desires of a larger proportion of the congregation than carelessly curated or unthinkingly repeated worship does.

CURATING WORSHIP

Curation isn't about any particular shape or style of worship, or about the inclusion or exclusion of any particular element. I would hope that by the end of this book you will be thinking about ways to improve the worship you design and curate, but the elements you start with next week may look exactly like those you started with last week, and the week before. And that's okay. Curation is as much about the attitude you bring to the worship event as it is about the elements of worship. It's the understanding you bring from the process of asking the questions described in the previous chapter—questions about who makes up your worshiping community and how you can help them engage with God in ways that will nurture and sustain them. But when you adopt the worship-curation model, some things will change right away.

Since the curator oversees the whole scope of the worship event, people participating in that event need to know how they relate to the curator. This is not a control or authority relationship. This is not a worship leader given a new name and more power to dominate. The number of songs that will be sung, and where the offering will be, and when the children will leave are decided by the community itself, or, perhaps, by a senior pastor. It's not the role of the curator to move the community into a new form of worship—unless that is what the community has asked for. The curator at a gallery is not the artist or the gallery owner. She doesn't take up a paint brush or chisel. Her responsibility is to do the best she can for the audience with the parameters and the works of art given to her. The worship curator is no different. Her role is to take what she is given—the elements of worship expected by her given community—and reshape where she is able and thinks it necessary in order to present these elements to the congregation at worship. To do this, she has to have a reasonable idea of what elements she has to curate. She will take this and curate, pruning and adding from her own aggregation of creative possibilities.

When the elements are tightly controlled by other forces, her role might involve little more than creating transitions between elements and setting up the space. This is still a significant contribution to the worship event. At other times, she may have more space to be creative with some of the elements of the service. Done with sensitivity, wisdom, and humility (three essential character traits of any worship curator), even a seemingly minimal contribution can have a deep impact on individuals and a community at worship.

Curation: The Glue That Holds It All Together

Curating Community Worship

Let me illustrate what curation looks like with an example from a community-worship event I worked on. (I consider *community* worship the week-by-week worship that usually is done in the same place, primarily for Christians. Other types are *transitional* and *guerrilla* worship. These will be discussed more fully in chapter 10.) One Palm Sunday, I curated morning and evening services for the Vineyard Church I'm connected to. There were seventy adults at each service. The church meets in a converted-warehouse setting with white walls, movable chairs, and no religious symbols. It's not a large space, and it has several pillars in unhelpful places and a low concrete ceiling. Not the most worship-inducing setting, but it's what I had to work with.

Apart from choosing the songs we'd sing, the whole service was mine to curate. In addition, I would be preaching the sermon and talking about Palm Sunday. I would be following their standard minimalist order of service:

- Prelude—live music by the worship band
- Welcome by the song leader
- Single worship song
- Children leave for their program
- Thirty-five minutes of sung worship
- Notices
- Preaching
- More sung worship and prayer perhaps with a call for ministry (that is, praying and laying on of hands)

Since it was my first time curating worship for this community and because I was working with a community that knew little to nothing about the church year, I made only minor alterations to the order of elements in the worship event. I decided I would introduce them to the church year, put Palm Sunday in context, preach, and offer just four simple stations[16] that would facilitate responses to the preaching. (This would equate to the usual call for ministry.)

I set up my stations carefully, thinking about how people would flow through them, what kind of instructions would be provided, what materials I would need, and so on. I wanted people to feel comfortable in the context of an altered order of service, so I was careful not to make too many changes to the usual layout of the space. I removed junk from the areas around the stations, tidied up the curtains, lampstands, and coffee tables. I tested the light switches to see what lighting suited the mood I hoped to create. I was curating the space and environment I was given as effectively and as simply as possible, always aware of the compromise between what I wanted to achieve and the limits of how far I could push this congregation.

I inserted a call to worship after the first song, including a short ritual in which we lit a Christ candle and did a responsive reading. The band played the rest of their set as usual. So we started as expected. Nothing too different. My sermon, in the regular slot, began with a brief comment about the church year. Then I hung a clothesline. I had a basket of clothes representing the major festivals and days in the church year and asked people to tell me where on the line they thought each item should hang. I had deliberately chosen just six or seven major church festivals—I wanted to teach them, not humiliate them. I concluded that section with a spoken segue suggesting that the value of the church year was that it helped us to think deliberately about the main parts of the Christian story, including Palm Sunday.

The sermon centered on a contemporary work of art by Jan Hynes called *Entering the City*. It's her interpretation of Jesus entering Jerusalem, set in her hometown of Townsville in Australia. Everyone had a small color copy of the work. I projected it on the front screen and a large print hung at the rear of the space.

Following the sermon, which was a monologue but shorter than usual, I invited people to respond by using one of the stations I had set up at the front, center, and sides of the room (see below)—these are the areas people would usually come to for altar calls and prayer. I explained what stations were and how to use them. I also mentioned that they had the option of staying seated and rereading the biblical text. (This gave people who weren't quite comfortable with the station idea a way to opt out yet remain involved in the event.)

I had chosen to use water instead of wine for communion for several reasons: it levels the playing field between those who are and are not able to drink wine; it has connections to the biblical stories of water becoming wine and springs of living water, it also reminds us of people in prisons and those without enough clean water. After explaining why we were using water and saying the words of institution (not usually done in this community), I played some ambient electronic music, and people moved around.

I waited until it seemed like everyone had finished moving, let the last track fade out, and led the community in prayer. We then stood and read a benediction off the screen together (they don't usually have a benediction), and that was it.

This is what was in their handouts, along with images and Luke 19:28-48, the biblical text for Palm Sunday.

STATIONS

Intro: Have a quick read through the possibilities. Find something that catches your attention. They are in no particular order. You may choose to use one, several, all, or none of them to guide your reflections.

Move around the space when you are ready.

Station 1: Sit with Jesus: Bread and Water
(The elements were set on a large, low table so people had to kneel to serve themselves. We provided jugs of ice water, midsized glasses, and a full loaf of bread. I wanted to create a sense of graciousness and abundance in the form of good food and a long, refreshing drink of water.)

After you have taken bread and water, reflect on what is ahead for you in the next week, month, year. What do you most need from Jesus today? Clarity? Understanding? Courage? Insight? Wisdom? Forgiveness? Strength? As you share the meal in community with your fellow followers of Jesus, encounter the risen Christ and receive what you need to move forward.

Station 2: *Entering the City*, Jan Hynes.
Look carefully at the painting—on the screen, the large print, or in the Lenten Reflections booklet. What do you think the artist is trying to say about the event? Where would you put yourself in the painting? Mark that spot on the painting in your booklet. Is this where you want to be? Mark where

you would like to be. What needs to happen for this movement to take place?

Station 3: Expectations

What about following Jesus isn't what you expected? Is this good? Bad? Does it matter? Does it say more about you than about Jesus, or the other way around? Do you need to change anything? Write a note to Jesus, or to yourself about this. When you have finished, burn it and move on. (We provided small pieces of paper and pencils for writing, and a large wok for the burning.)

Station 4: Crying for the City

O Lord of all encounters, forgive me for being a spectator.
I watch the passing parade by hiding in the crowd.
I would rather avoid the cost of getting involved, of
    standing out, of being noticed.
I say my hosannas and watch the city die.
I wave my palm branches and go on my way.
O God of the lowly, teach me how to feel with others
Let me share in the hurt and hunger of the street.
Help me to turn my apathy and distractedness into
    creative care.
Renew me with the experience of your grace and the
    reality of your mercy.
Through Jesus Christ, who is my Lord as well as my
    save-r, Amen. (Source unknown. Modified)

Light a candle as a symbol of your prayer for yourself and the city. (We provided candles and sandtrays.)

People appeared to be completely engaged, and the feedback was extremely positive. The format was a bit different from what I might have done if the community was used to using stations and understood the church year. Either way, it is the role of the curator to take responsibility for the whole space and what happens in it as we enable the community to engage with God.

Curating a regular weekly worship event at Cityside Church in Auckland or Urban Seed Church in Melbourne would call for a different set of elements and expectations. Both of these communities have the expectation of participation by a variety of people leading different segments of the worship, and stationed responses in the service are commonplace. In these communities, the curator's job involves managing the segues between all of these people and elements. So while the order of service is set in quite a liturgical way—a prelude followed by a call to worship, a song or meditation, a prayer of confession, and so on—whoever is leading that segment can do so however she wants. So the prelude might be a recorded track off the Top Ten, the call to worship might be a ritual action, and the prayer of confession might be a responsive reading, each led by a different person. Establishing a flow from one element to the next is a difficult task to do well and requires quite specific skills and intuition. A good curator makes it look easy. In fact, she will be invisible and not even noticed.

Curating Transitional Worship

The next example of the curator's role in community worship moves toward what I call *transitional* worship. (This will be explained fully in chapter 10.) This worship event involved a fully curated space as well as a fully curated order of service. It was Good Friday at the 150-year-old downtown Baptist church of which I am a part. I rewrote a 2006 service I had cowritten and cocurated with Cheryl Lawrie and others in Melbourne. I wanted to make it more overtly biblical and make it a better fit for a conservative congregation that had zero experience with stations.

The Baptist church building is old and has a semicircular balcony like a theater and fixed theater-like seats in a large arc on a tiered floor. The main floor seats 350. To make the space smaller and more intimate, I hung a five-foot-wide white vinyl apron from the balcony to create a kind of "back wall" for the main floor. It also served as a screen where I projected a video clip in two places. This "wall" stopped a few feet short of the floor, so people had to stoop slightly to get into the space.

The large main platform is on two levels. On the bottom level, I spread 1700 pounds of crushed white sea ice and 100 pounds of 5-pound ice blocks. Above the pristine white ice hung a barbed wire crown of thorns with eight red icicles dripping onto the white ice below. I lit the red icicles with spotlights, and they shone like red patent leather. Around the front and side areas of the platform were five stations repeated three times each. I lit the space with six ultraviolet lights as well as some light spilling from the projector and through the blind-covered windows. It wasn't dark enough for the ultraviolet light to give its full effect of making white paper and cotton clothing glow vividly, but it worked well enough.

The event didn't follow a normal order of service. This was a one-off special service, so I could get away with that. People had been informed through the newsletter for several weeks that this would be an art-installation-based service of reflection. People entered and were given a handout with information on the order of the service, the stations, and all the reflection questions for the event. They were seated for the first twenty minutes of readings, then the stations were brought out in a ritualized way by a person dressed in a hooded CSI-type white suit.

After a careful explanation of ways to explore the space and reference to the printed instructions in the handout, people were invited to move around the space and engage with God through the stations and the responses they called for. The same black-and-white video loop ran throughout, and a variety of music tracks ran in the background. After an hour, the service ended with U2's "Wake Up Dead Man" and a responsive reading. People were asked to move out quietly and not disturb those who wished to stay in the space a bit longer.

There was a lot of preparation work to make sure the space worked well, that people could physically move around the stations, and that the order of service would flow easily. In particular, I wanted to make sure people were prepared with enough biblical content and context to engage with the stations. The responses from the apparently fully engaged, mostly older adult congregation of 150 were overwhelmingly positive. This may have been their first experience of this style of worship, but they loved it and met God through it.

I realize how frustrating it may be for curators who are not yet able to curate worship experiences like this for their communities. But curating is about going on a personal and communal journey with your people. It's about leading the congregation to engage with God, not about me showing how much I know or how creative I can be. It's slow, and you may encounter many potholes of criticism and failure along the way. But the journey is as important as any destination and, like any journey, starts by taking the first small step.

Almost a year after the Good Friday service described above, I curated an allocated twenty-five-minute slot in a regular Sunday morning service at the same church. I was to introduce Lent—particularly Ash Wednesday—in the context of communion. I would not be responsible for any more of the service than my part. So I took a curator's approach to my slot.

During the week before the service, I negotiated with the generous and gracious senior pastor to have people come out from their theater seats and be served communion at the front and back. While unusual, this had been done once before. There would be more than 300 people present, spread over the upstairs as well as downstairs areas, which made for some logistical challenges. In consultation with the pastoral staff, we decided that there would be five pairs of servers downstairs and four upstairs. One person in each pair would hold the bread plate and the cups tray, while the second person would offer the imposition of ashes, (the making of a cross sign with ash on the forehead of worshipers). My intention was to do a very brief introduction to the church year, move to an extended explanation of Lent and Ash Wednesday, and use communion as the response to that. Communion and the ashing would be opportunities to commit to following a Lenten journey of renewed commitment to following Jesus.

When I arrived for the service, the pastor told me that the church administrator had found it difficult to find enough people to serve communion as a number had refused to serve when they discovered ashing would be part of the service. It wasn't that they felt uncomfortable doing the ashing, they were opposed to it happening at all! No reasons were given nor, unfortunately, asked for. The senior pastor had been fielding complaints for several days but had chosen not to burden me with them. We talked about the possible ways forward. I offered to withdraw the ashing if that was what he wanted. He wasn't sure what he wanted. I offered a compromise where I would be the only person offering ashing, and the communion serving pairs would stay as arranged but serve one of the elements each. He agreed, and we got set up for the service.

As I said earlier, the role of the curator is to find the best ways of encouraging people to engage with God. It is also to make sure the environment is safe for all participants. The balance between risk and safety is a shifting one. I felt that ashing was entirely appropriate and would be significant for at least some people. I also wanted to move the community just a little bit in its understanding and acceptance of what are very ancient Christian traditions. I was also loathe to bow to the lowest common denominator, despite some people clearly feeling uncomfortable with what I was intending to do.

When it came time for communion, about 25 out of perhaps 280 people came to my station. As I anointed them with eucalyptus oil mixed with ashes, I said, "You are dust re-created in the image of God. Go in peace." I could sense that this was a significant moment for many, and, following the service, I heard nothing from the critics but much from people for whom the content, communion, or ashing had been meaningful.

TRAINING A WORSHIP CURATOR

I hope these examples serve to give you some idea of what curation might mean in different settings, and that the role of the worship curator isn't an easy one. An article on the Princeton Review website describing the characteristics and training needed to make a good art gallery curator says:

> Both graduate education and practical experience are required for people who wish to become curators. Aside from an extensive knowledge of history and art, it is useful to have a basic understanding of chemistry, restoration techniques, museum studies, and even physics and public relations. Curators must have basic skills in aesthetic design, organizational behavior, business, fund-raising, and publicity. Many employers look favorably on foreign language skills as

well. To become a collection manager or a curatorial assistant, a master's degree is required. To become a curator at a national museum, a PhD is required, as is about five years of field experience. The market is competitive, and academic standards are very high. Useful graduate degrees include restoration science, curatorship, art history, history, chemistry, and business administration. Nearly all curators find it helpful to engage in continuing education. Research and publication in academic journals are important for advancement in the field.[17]

While those criteria are hardly appropriate for a worship curator, they indicate the seriousness with which agencies outside the church take the role. How seriously does the church generally take designing worship?

Curator Suzanne Page made a comment that I find especially applicable to the art of curating worship. She said:

> I don't like to put myself into the spotlight, but I like to illuminate the backstage. What I suggest is actually very demanding. It takes an effort not to emphasize your own subjectivity, and to let the [worship] itself be at the center.... To a certain degree it is a question of learning to be vulnerable. . . . It's about forgetting everything you think that you know, and even allowing yourself to get lost.... [W]hat I am after is a form of concentration that suddenly turns into its opposite, being available for a true alternative adventure.[18]

I long for the day when churches will take the role of their worship curators as seriously as the art world does, the day when seminaries and theological colleges will offer training in worship curation and sponsor "curator at large" and "curator in residence" positions. In the meantime, you will need to make up your own training schedule.

While a good worship curator requires a different set of educational and work experiences than a museum or gallery curator does, the task is no less difficult, complex, or serious. In particular, I believe an attention to detail is important—it's difficult to curate well if you are not a detail person. I think it is the details that make or break worship. I've seen many great ideas executed poorly. If participants don't understand what you're asking them to do in relation to your fabulously creative idea, if they can't read the beautifully designed and intricately folded handout you have given them because the font is too small for the lighting level, if they are in a building that is bitterly cold, then much of what you are curating is wasted. It comes down to being able to put yourself in the shoes of a participant and to imagine what each step of the worship experience might be like for him.

In my experience, good worship curators are people who are pastoral in approach, who have at least some theological insight if not education, who are intuitive and teachable. They don't have big egos. In fact, a successful worship event is one in which they are almost invisible.

THE CHALLENGES OF CURATION

The task of a worship curator in our time and culture is complex. Our relationship to what were once considered basic images and symbols of the Christian faith keeps changing and needs to be recontextualized. The cross, for example, is strongly associated with Christianity—so much so that in Muslim countries, the Red Cross disaster-relief agency is known as the Red Crescent. At the time of Jesus, the cross was an instrument of state execution, a sign of disgrace and scandal. The followers of Jesus picked it up as an act of subversion, upending the values of the empire. It was a sign that followers of Jesus were willing to follow him in suffering, that the empire had no real say over their lives. Christendom took the cross on as a symbol of power and honor, a badge to be worn proudly. By the time of the Crusades, taking up your cross didn't imply a willingness to die but a readiness to kill! In our day, it has become a fashion accessory. Madonna is reported as saying, "Crucifixes are sexy because there's a naked man on them!"[19]

The changing perceptions of and uses of the cross remind us how difficult it is to curate worship these days. It is difficult because we can mess things up much more easily. There is no waterproof, fireproof model laid out for us to follow, only nuances, emphases, and guidelines that can leave us struggling and uncertain. And they can get us criticized. That's why it is so much easier and safer to use the same book, sing the same songs, and speak the same words week after week.

Worship curators, particularly young people working in older congregations, need the help of mentors to help them navigate the complexities of the contemporary church. Yes, we need emerging leaders, but we also need emerged leaders who will work alongside them. The tech-savvy twenty-year-old can teach and learn from a veteran of forty years of pastoral leadership, and the veteran has much to teach and learn from the beginner.

Trust is an important ingredient in this. The curator and community enter into a symbiotic relationship that requires each to know they can be trusted and are trusted by the other. This can only come about over time by working together as equals and sharing successes and failures.

It's also difficult to be a worshiper in worship you are curating. Worship curating requires a focus and attentiveness to what is happening for other people. In a fully curated, ambient, stationed space, it is often possible to engage with a few of the stations. But the curator only rarely experiences these events with the openness needed for true spiritual reflection and change. If you want to worship, it's best to find an event curated by someone else. You might also find, like I do, that in many cases the preparations for a worship event become your worship experience.

No one person will have all the ideal characteristics of a worship curator. I don't; you don't. A good curator will find ways and people to compensate for her weaknesses. I'm always looking for someone who is good with language and for a great graphic designer. I need long lists to help me get through an event I've curated because I am prone to forgetting small details. Other curators need to work with someone who is more pastorally aware or who understands theology better than they do. All curators need to be on a journey of personal transformation.

What I have described in this chapter is a relatively high-level view of curating. It's a bit more than might be expected of, say, someone who's been asked to find a prayer of confession for Sunday. But even if you're responsible for that small task, you can enhance what you do by seeing your role through the eyes of a worship curator. The attitude or processes of a curator should not be reserved only for full-blown worship events. They apply in smaller, equally significant ways to every element of a worship event.

Anyone can describe him or herself as a worship curator—the more the term is used the better. But it is not just a trendy term. It carries real meaning and implications for those who use it. Those of us in the church are very good at taking a term or process from the surrounding culture and skimming the surface of it, sucking off the icing and leaving the cake behind. By developing the term *worship curator*, I want people to take the design and preparation of worship more seriously and to understand more deeply what they are doing.

I want worship curators to put together more transformative and engaging worship than they ever did as a worship leaders. At the very least, use the term with intent and to remind yourself that you are on a deliberate journey toward becoming the best curator of worship you can be.

4

A New Language for Worship: Applying the Philosophy of Curation

We come from far and wide;
We have our own stories to tell who we are
Stories of places and people and experiences
Tales of discovery and disappointment.

Somewhere between there and here,
God has become a part of our adventure;
Part of our walking and speaking and breathing,
In us and through us and before us.

We have joined our lives with the story of Christ,
And begun to act as if it were true;
Taking the words to be gospel,
And the sound of them to be the breath of life.

Sometime between then and now,
God has come to dwell among us,
Breathing the Spirit into our hearts
So that we may see and hear and feel.

With our friends and fellow travelers,
We have measured our days by the kingdom
And our nights by the joy of salvation;
Seeking what is lost within us.

We are the substance of Christ's dreaming
The firstfruits and the foretaste
The small and suffering people
In whom Christ has pleased to dwell.

But we are also the lost children;
The straying sheep and the dishonest servants,
The rich young fools and the rock-bearing elders,
The timid followers and the traitorous disciples.

We often forget the story which came to us,
Preferring order to uncertainty;
Orthodoxy to love,
And religious piety to unmerited grace.

Come to us again, Lord Jesus,
And whisper your words of welcome;
Fill our hearts with reckless wonder,
And our minds with splendid nonsense.

Awake in us the dream of the kingdom;
Resurrect our dead and perished visions;
Alert us to the heaven in our midst;
And quicken us to laugh and love.

Here we have no lasting city;
No temple nor castle nor club;
Here we have no religious refuge
In which to hide from your gratuitous chaos.

So make us to be the dwelling of Christ,
The holy shelter in which the flame may burn;
That the story may go on and the truth be told,
And mercy come to your good earth.
Amen.[20]

Trompe l'oeil is two-dimensional painting done with such attention to detail that to many observers it appears three dimensional. When it comes to art, this or any other, what you see depends largely on how you look, what you expect to see, what you bring to your looking, and where you stand while you're looking. The same is true of worship.

The alternative-worship movement that arose in the United Kingdom and—almost simultaneously—in New Zealand in the early 1990s was built around some clear values and practices. While these were clarified in retrospect rather than articulated beforehand, they were, and remain, commonly held and strongly committed to by alternative-worship practitioners. In 2005, attempting to explain what alternative worship was about, Steve Collins, British alternative-worship commentator and practitioner, posted this list on his website at http://www.alternativeworship.org. While it is a long list, I include it to describe in detail both the reactionary and visionary natures of this movement in a country where a well-established liturgical-church event was the norm. For him, alternative worship is:

- Christians reinventing faith expression for themselves within their own cultural settings
- a response to postmodern Western society and cultural change
- faith expression within culture, not in a parallel "Christian" culture
- reconsideration of all inherited church forms and structures, including recent modernising ones
- rediscovery of ancient and alternative Christian traditions as resources for the present and future
- paradigm shift from centralised into networked forms of church
- not intended to transition people into existing forms of church
- not an attempt to reach particular social or cultural groups
- not about making Christianity appear cool or fashionable
- not a restyling of existing forms and structures
- authenticity—faith expression that truly represents the people who make and take part in it
- faith as journey, to be facilitated rather than controlled
- giving people space for their own encounter with God
- an exploration of creativity—in everyone, not just a gifted few
- risk-taking, experimental—openness to failure and mistakes

- holistic—life not divided into sacred and secular
- any part of our lives and abilities as potential material for faith expression
- participation—involvement encouraged, passive consumption discouraged
- minimal exclusion—shaped by whoever gets involved
- consensus—not one person imposing their direction
- low threshold of permission—in general if you want to do something go ahead
- high quality, as good as we can make it—culturally aware
- awareness of ourselves as part of God's creation, and a concern for its welfare
- the entire expression of the faith community seen as 'church' not just one event
- reluctance to draw boundaries that determine who or what is in or out of God's kingdom
- openness to God's presence in any area of life or culture
- high level of trust in people's ability to deliver appropriate content
- event led by many people not one or two
- relaxed, informal
- congregation are active participants
- rituals and liturgies—ancient e.g. Holy Communion, or newly created
- moving around the space
- interaction with installations and artworks

- periods when people can do different things at the same time
- learning by exploration and interaction, not located in a single 'teaching' slot
- [usually no] sermons or didactic teaching
- [no] sitting in one place all the time
- [no] worship bands, choirs or organs
- [no] one person at the front directing everything
- [no] PowerPoint presentations
- no pews or rows of seats
- no pulpit
- no stage
- non-directional space—no front to face, things happen all around
- soft seating, beanbags, sit or lie on floor
- cafe spaces—chairs and tables, sofas, food and drink
- intimate lighting—spotlights, candles, TVs, projections
- installations and artworks
- ambient music—as background to everything including speech and prayer
- ambient video—relevant to event content but not attention-grabbing
- technology and media used as environment or art as well as presentation tools
- venue may not be existing church building[21]

Rather than picking out a number of items and measuring your worship life against that selection, it is the combined weight of those values that is important. It's definitely not a list of instructions to follow!

In the British-, Australian-, and New Zealand-based alternative-worship movement of the 1990s, we were largely reacting against an institutional form of church that didn't connect with our lives or allow us real participation in what was happening in the worship event. In the United Kingdom, that was done predominantly by young adults who enjoyed the rave and dance scene. At the other side of the world, people like me were looking for church life that connected with the other pieces of our lives and could potentially do the same for our unchurched friends. Churches that met in nonchurch buildings with frontless, pewless worship spaces and multimedia capabilities were the reactionary norm.

It worried me that even after five or six years of extremely hard and constant work, all the groups I knew of, including Parallel Universe that I was part of, were still small. If we had thirty participants beyond those of us organizing the event, it was a big night. For many groups, it wasn't much more than the organizing team. The generally monthly worship event was often stunning—creative, participatory, engaging, transformative—and I loved it wherever in the world I encountered it. But the cost-benefit ratio was very high. Often it was unsustainable, and many groups flared brightly and burned out over the decade.

Gradually, I came to the conclusion that unless we saw our movement as one providing alternative church and not just alternative worship, we had no future. I was critical of the many groups in the United Kingdom, Australia, and New Zealand who were, in my opinion, quite content to stay small and indulge in spiritual masturbation. Despite not being in any way a disciple of the church-growth movement, I reluctantly concluded that unless our communities were growing numerically, we weren't fulfilling our mission as the church.

Still, I couldn't understand why a style of worship that I and many others loved wasn't bulging at the seams with people at every service.

I still don't really understand why this was the case, except that we were not offering much beyond a worship event, and we were quite reactionary, perhaps even elitist at times, and probably unnecessarily critical of inherited churches.

Alongside Parallel Universe, I had been leading a decreasing group of people over at Cityside Baptist Church. Because I was working full time (and then some), involvement in these dual projects became unsustainable. Both took too much time, and both showed little return. So, not without pain and some conflict among the Parallel Universe team, I took what I was doing and had learned there about worship, mission, and cultural engagement, and melded it into the worship life and values of Cityside Baptist Church, which at that time had about twenty adults at worship on a good day.

Until that time, our Sunday worship event looked like any other Baptist service of the day: multiple songs of praise and worship, preaching, notices, and offering, all framed by a call to worship and Benediction. The congregation would sit in rows of pews listening to what was said and being led from the pulpit.

Cityside was one of the first church communities anywhere to work out alternative-worship principles in a "regular" church context. We met weekly in a traditional church building and were part of a mainstream denomination (despite public criticism of what we were doing by other churches in that "family"). I am extremely grateful for this journey, for the Cityside community who came with me, and for the people around the world with whom I developed friendships along the way. It's a wonderful international community to be part of.

I still find the values and practices of the alternative-worship movement inspiring and useful touchstones. The original questions remain foundational for me. Yet I want to move beyond them to values and language that reflect more closely what worship can become Sunday by Sunday.

BUILDING A VOCABULARY

I have come to find that I need a language that works for weekly worship events as well as the kind of events the alternative- and emerging-worship movements provide. The questions of curation discussed in chapter 3—What is church? What is worship?—are just the beginning. To truly develop a sense of worship as an art form, we need to rediscover the meaning of some of the terms we have in our vocabulary for worship as well as add a few new ones. Many of you will already have a good working vocabulary with which to begin but need to develop language that is more appropriate in the culture in which you are seeking to offer spiritual sustenance and formation. Others will have a very limited vocabulary that needs to be expanded before you are able to develop adequate language about worship.

In the realm of worship curation, there are a host of terms that I have found necessary when talking and thinking about worship. I have used these terms both in my own understanding of what I hope to do as a curator and in my conversations with others, and I bring them to the curation process. For the purposes of this book, I will discuss these terms under three major headings: "Curation Philosophy," "Curation Practice," and "Community Engagement," but there is considerable overlap. Some of the terms are quite technical and take a bit of thinking through in order to understand how they might apply to worship. Others are more familiar and lighter in weight. Most are not terms normally associated with worship or church life. I don't even expect that you will remember or use them all. I offer them to help you to think more seriously, more deeply, and more significantly about the role you have as a worship curator and to understand the significance of what you are involved in. I want you to begin to build a vocabulary that will provide you with a new language for describing and designing corporate public worship.

CURATION PHILOSOPHY

In the broad sense, *curation* involves a philosophical shift in how we think about worship. Where worship has often been thought of in rather closed, even private terms, curation calls for a new sensibility, one that brings with it words and ideas we don't often consider when talking about worship, such as:

- participation
- open-endedness
- slow worship
- integrity
- failure
- questions

Participation

When I ask pastoral leaders whether they allow and encourage participation in worship events, nearly every one of them replies with an adamant "Yes!" The reality is far different, at least by my understanding of participation.

Most worship events benefit the preacher. She uses her theological education to help her understand the weekly biblical text. She takes a few days to read commentaries and other resources on the text; then she sifts through these findings to create a fifteen- to forty-five-minute verbal monologue that gets poured over the captive congregation. They hear it once, but the preacher has heard it and worked it over many times.

If worship is about giving people the opportunity to respond to God in ways that nurture them spiritually and enable them to better engage with the world in which they live, that benefit needs to be spread more widely. The only way I know to do this is to build a culture of participation at all levels of church and mission, and especially in worship.

Participation doesn't just mean having the congregation sing or pray together. It means making the entire worship event the product of guided or curated involvement—an art installation where the elements of worship are the artifacts. It is worship where a variety of people from all backgrounds, ages, levels of commitment, learning styles, education, and stages of spiritual formation contribute creatively to the content, leadership, and shaping of the worship event. That's participation. Maybe that sounds like a recipe for disaster. "What about the quality of the worship?" you ask. "Won't it suffer? God demands our best, right? How can we risk giving God anything less than a practiced, polished worship service? Surely our worship will slip badly under this model."

Now might be a good time for me to declare that I'm antiexcellence. I'm antiexcellence in church life generally, and I'm particularly antiexcellence in worship. I know some branches of the church preach a strongly proexcellence message, but I can't help wondering if excellence is a cultural value rather than a biblical one.

I'm sure someone could quote a First Testament verse referring to the excellence required of artisans working on the temple in King Solomon's time, but I think they'd be hard-pressed to squeeze one from the Second Testament, particularly from the lips of Jesus. I don't think excellence in worship is a goal that has any biblical support.

This isn't to say that excellence in church life is always bad, but a preoccupation with it is never good. Excellence comes at a very high price in terms of time and money. It leads to performance and is almost always applied to music, drama, and video presentations done to the congregation by those elevated on the stage. Like the preacher, those doing the singing and preparing the drama become excellent at what they do, whole those in the pews are consistently reduced to being consumers. In their hearts, they know that they are not quite as spiritual or worthy as those who worship on their behalf.

Don't misunderstand me. I'm not against excellence per se, just its elevation to sainthood. In fact I'm really not so much antiexcellence as proparticipation. I believe church life should be about participation. But performance gets in the way of true participation, and a pursuit of excellence always ends up being about performance. If excellence is a primary goal, then the weak, the timid, the depressed, the disabled, the unskilled, the sick, the introverted, the overweight, the less attractive, the poor, and the untalented aren't going to get a look in. They'll be relegated to being spectators for someone else's worship performance. From this perspective, excellence doesn't look so good. In fact, it sounds quite un-Christlike, almost evil. How can a process and a value that excludes large sections of a worshiping community from active participation be named in any other way? Jesus had some pretty harsh words for those in his day who devised ways of making it tough for ordinary people to worship God—something about them being as spiritually alive as spruced-up tombs, and not being able to see clearly because they had something in their eyes.

Worship leaders need to open their eyes, get off the stage and out of the front rows and sit at the back of their auditoriums from time to time, so they can experience what worship feels like for the rest of the congregation. Often only people in the first few rows are actively involved in what's going on, while those sitting further back might not sing, or read along, or tune in at all.

Presbyterian liturgical scholar, Craig Erickson, argues that truly participatory worship involves six key elements:

1. Silence (an interesting place to start!)
2. Involvement through the senses (not just a numb feeling in your backside!)

3. Lay leadership
4. Memorized verbal participation, for example, saying the Lord's Prayer together
5. Prophetic verbal participation, for example, where individuals creatively sum up and name the concerns of the congregation before God in prayer
6. Spontaneous participation[22]

It's a useful checklist and a reminder of the depth and breadth that's possible when there is true participation.

If I am to be consistent with my earlier definitions of *church* and *worship*, then what I do in the worship events I design and curate must be about supporting people in their following of Christ in the world through their responding to ongoing encounters with God. Everything else flows from that. We come together as followers of Jesus, so we can share stories of the successes and failures of our life in the world, find encouragement and support in being with each other and in worshiping God together, and separate to follow Christ and serve his world through another week. What we need to value most is community, our relationships with one another. That's why I'm proparticipation in corporate public community worship, regardless of how excellent or poor that participation might be. It's only in being open to as much participation as possible that community can be built. The prayer of confession I lead the church in might not be the best theology, it might not be the most polished performance, it might even offend some people with its awkward language or content, but it will reflect who I am and where my relationship with God is. You'll get to know me a little more than you did before, and maybe you'll even get to make your confession. In preparing that prayer, I will have learned something about following Jesus and the traditions of the church and Scripture. I'll have taken a little more responsibility for my own spiritual formation.

At Cityside Church, a number of people participate each week by curating and leading an element of the worship event. They can do this in any way, using any medium and content they wish. One morning a young man named Warrick stood to lead us in the prayer of confession. He said, "I was phoned during the week to remind me I was on the prayer of confession. My flatmate slipped a note under my door that read, 'Warrick, you're on the prayer of concession this week.' So I am going to lead us in a prayer of concession." My heart sank as I anticipated what might follow. I was wrong. Warrick prayed, "Dear God, we concede that we are not the people you want us to be. We concede that you are right, that your way is right, that you have the right-of-way, that you are correct. We yield to your mercy and to your forgiveness. We allow your forgiveness to wash us and to cleanse us. We concede our lives to you. Amen." I was rightly humbled. His participation demonstrated excellence.

If any worship—emerging, alternative, charismatic, evangelical, reformed, or any other genre—is more about *what* and *how* it is done than *why* it is done and if high quality—whether of video loops, music, or singing—becomes more important than transformative encounters with God that allow people to follow Jesus more closely in their world and subculture, then this worship isn't worthy of being called *worship*.

I've said I'm antiexcellence in church life, and I am. But I'm proexcellence in my life and in the life of every person in any congregation I am part of. I want to be the best I can be at what I do and who I am. I want the same for everyone where I worship. I want what we offer as worship to be as good as it can be. I want every individual who participates in leading any aspect of our worship to be as good as possible at doing so. But I'll take participation over excellence every time. I hope our worship and wider life together will produce confident, maturing followers of Jesus Christ who live creatively, courageously, and justly in the chaotic emerging culture. I hope they will be maturing followers of Jesus Christ, able to interpret their faith in the marketplace of life. If together we produce excellence in some of our worship events along the way, that's wonderful, but it's not our goal.

Open-endedness

When an art installation curator has completed her task, she has, to a large extent, lost control. She is not able to tell people what to think, or what conclusions to draw, or what to feel. In the same way the artist gives up control once he completes his work, so the gallery curator can now only watch as people come and go and comment on what the installation means to them. I had no real idea of what the paint-pond artists had in mind when they curated the installation I experienced with my daughter, and I came away with my own ideas. All curators are in that situation.

The ability and courage to live with open-endedness in worship is one of the most difficult—and perhaps most important—habits to acquire. Nothing delights me more than to hear someone talking after a worship event about how God has spoken to him about a particular aspect of Scripture or an area of his life when I know we never came near to addressing that particular idea in the worship event. If the church is about sustaining people in their following of Christ in the world and worship is providing spaces where those people can encounter God in ways that will sustain them, then I don't need to be concerned about ensuring that everyone goes away "knowing" the same thing.

Open-endedness is another way of describing the work of the Spirit of God in worship. It is the Spirit curating my curation, applying the biblical text or theme to every person in ways that are specific to their needs, ways I could never hope to be aware of or achieve. Open-endedness is giving the biblical text room to breathe.

At the same time, open-endedness is not an excuse for shallowness or lack of preparation. It is acknowledging that God may speak to someone about issues unrelated to anything I have thought about in relation to the worship event. It's about allowing space in the worship for that to happen. This may come in the form of silence, allowing for movement around the space, or providing a variety of stations or ways to respond during the event. It's the recognition that as curator I am a provider and shaper of context as well as content; and that both are equally important.

Earlier, I quoted Mike Riddell's response to Hotere's *Black Phoenix* installation. I saw this installation twice in two different settings. The first was in a huge, very high-ceilinged, open room. The blackened prow and timbers were laid out along one wall and on the floor in front. There was nothing else in the room. We entered the room along the wall opposite the installation. The second time, it was installed in a much smaller space with some timbers missing and other works in the same space. My response was very different. Same artifacts, different curation, and, therefore, different outcomes. And I would guess that neither response was what Hotere or the curators had in mind.

We experience open-endedness every Sunday in our churches, whether we intend to or not. If you are a pastoral leader or preacher, or even if you discuss the service or sermon with friends after church, you know that two people can hear the same words, read the same text, experience the same worship, and come away with entirely different messages. These are not necessarily conflicting understandings of the text, but rather different ways in which God has spoken to them.

As a pastor, I am delighted whenever anyone in my community of faith encounters God. Whether that encounter comes through the three points I drew from the Scripture in my good Baptist sermon, or a cartoon in the newsletter, I don't mind. The purpose of the worship is to curate a setting in which an encounter can take place, not to dictate the outcome.

Open-endedness is about allowing room for the Holy Spirit to move; it's also about a willingness to raise questions without always giving answers, to not feel it necessary to tell the whole story every time. Sermons that are too neat, and have every question answered, and every rough patch smoothed over don't allow people room to think for themselves. They suggest that the other questions people have are ones they shouldn't have. It's too easy to spend too much time worrying about being right and making sure we present the whole gospel every time, thereby spending too little time trusting the work of the Spirit.

Whenever I talk about participation and open-endedness, it is only a few minutes before someone asks the inevitable question, "But what about when someone says something from the front that isn't right/true? How do you control that?" My response is to ask them to elaborate on what that something not right or true might be. Most of the time their example is a point of doctrine and usually a pretty minor one. I hear that kind of error from the front at almost every service I attend anyway. The reality is there is no theological purity, and those who attempt it fall into the "scribes and Pharisees" camp about which Jesus had plenty of unfavourable things to say. A worship event should never be about theological purity. It should always be about ordinary people engaging their messy selves with the transformative person of the God who became flesh and lived in this messiness.

In the Cityside Church weekly newsletter, we ran a slogan that we lived by as a community of faith: "Thinking allowed, thinking aloud allowed." That applied to the preacher preaching as well as to anyone else.

Slow Worship

The slow-food movement is creeping around the world. Begun in Italy in 1986 by Carlo Petrini as a response to the negative impact of multinational food companies, the movement today has branches in some 130 countries over five continents. Slow food opposes the standardization of taste, protects the cultural identity of food, and seeks to safeguard traditional processing techniques. It involves valuing time to prepare, eat, and build community through food. It is sometimes criticized as being a pursuit of the wealthy, but slow food is about celebrating the connections that food can make with sustainable production and local-food traditions that are often lost in our economy. It's not about extravagance. It is quite the opposite.

Marcus Curnow in Melbourne has his roots in Cornwall, England, and is passionate about all things Cornish. He often makes Cornish pasties. (This is a pastry case with vegetables and meat inside it.) He gathers people to make and eat them as a community event. At a recent, gathering Marcus told me:

> Anyone who has shared Cornish pasties at my house will know that you are consuming much more than just the pasty. There is the story of our local organic food co-op, the ethical farming where the food came from, and the way the co-op has been a foundation for our local relationships. There is history—the famines of the 1840s that caused my forebears to come to Australia from Cornwall. There is learning how to chop and prepare the ingredients, to lay out

and crimp the pastry so it holds all the ingredients in. Then there's the stories of why this was important in the original context and the contemporary debates about what makes a pasty "proper" Cornish—sauce or no sauce and so on."

The slow-food movement has helped me reframe my understanding of what it means to be church. I want to explore a slow-worship movement, maybe even to be part of a "slow church." This doesn't mean singing more slowly or singing less—although both might be useful in some contexts! *Slow worship* means rather than picking up a prepackaged worship meal, we reflect on what we want to achieve in worship and take time, in our local setting, to use local resources that reflect the culture of our communities. It's avoiding the *When Harry Met Sally* syndrome mentioned earlier.

Slow food makes connections between consumption and production, something that is also vital for our worship. Pete Ward first drew my attention to this in his provocative and stimulating book, *Liquid Church*. He writes, "The church must change its emphasis from meeting people's spiritual needs to stimulating their desires. [Generally] church is set up to convince people of their need of God and then deliver salvation in response to this need."[23]

We live in a needs-centered culture. It is interesting to read the gospels with an eye toward observing when Jesus was meeting needs and when he was creating spiritual desire. Maybe he was capable of doing both simultaneously in a way we seem less capable of.

Slow worship assumes that people—inside and outside the church—are looking for an encounter with God. They might not give that phrase the same content as we would, but that's their desire—to encounter God. *Desire* is much deeper, less predictable and manageable, and more controversial than need. It can sound—but isn't necessarily so—much more consumer driven, as if needs have greater spiritual integrity and legitimacy than desires. But they don't. Our culture has made a religion out of meeting needs. Slow worship works on the assumption that everyone has some level of spiritual desire and that worship can and should be designed to engage with that desire.

Slow food opposes the standardization of taste. Slow worship should avoid "one-size-fits-all" ideas about church.

Slow food defends the need for consumer information about ingredients. Slow worship should arise from the needs and life experiences of the people.

Slow food protects cultural identities tied to food and gastronomic traditions. Slow worship continues and builds on the reframed traditions of the past.

Slow food safeguards foods and cultivation and processing techniques inherited from tradition. Slow worship should use and reframe rituals and traditions of the culture from the past.

Slow food involves taking time preparing and eating; eating with company; rediscovering the pleasure of eating and drinking; sourcing and preserving local foods, beverages, and themes; and community building. The connections with worship are obvious.

Slow worship is about understanding the principles behind what we do rather than just picking up a prepackaged worship meal and serving it up for our communities irrespective of their place in the world. Northern hemisphere Christmas traditions, songs, images, and rituals for deep winter don't translate well to New Zealand and Australia where the holiday is celebrated in the height of summer. Worship patterns don't even move easily from one side of town to another.

We assume that pretty much anyone can lead worship with little or no training. We generally expect our preachers to be trained, but anyone who looks good or can sing gets to lead the rest of the service. It's no wonder we have fast-food worship that looks and tastes the same the world over. It all comes out of the same book and takes almost no notice of ethnic variations, seasonal differences, or local tastes.

What I'm really suggesting is not just a slow-worship movement, but a slow-church movement, one that:

- opposes the standardization of worship, church life, and mission;
- defends the need for participation and involvement of all people;
- respects the traditions and rituals of the historic church;
- draws on the best of the past for the future;
- is strongly committed to the local community, cultures, and styles;
- doesn't serve up fast-food worship;
- builds community;
- enjoys hospitality;
- encourages creativity;
- is committed to justice.

Integrity

Integrity connects strongly with breadth and depth in worship. One of the main things that the alternative-worship movement taught us—and that the emerging-church movement needs to be cautious about—is that worship style and content should have integrity. In other words, both should be shaped by the worshiping community, not by what another group is doing or by the latest fad. New worship isn't about video loops and candles or art. It's about worship that is for the people, and by the people, and of the people.

I am not a goth, although I do mostly wear black. I am good at curating worship in a wide variety of contexts. If I were to put on a goth Eucharist like Karen Ward does at Sanctorum at the Church of the Apostles in Seattle, I would be dead in the water. The goths in the community would see through me in an instant. As a teenager, I was embarrassed when the elderly Youth for Christ director I worked under talked at a large public event for teenagers about how wonderful it was that the Beatles had become Christians. He demonstrated this "fact" by describing their new song, "My Sweet Lord." Anyone who was part of youth culture knew it was a song celebrating another deity.

The idea that we can curate worship for communities or subcultures of which we are not a part is anathema to me. This was a problem to me in the "seeker-driven" worship events I attended. They were intended for someone who wasn't there, but those of us who were there were still expected to worship God. In my experience, unchurched people are most likely to encounter God in a context where genuine worship is taking place. Certainly that worship should include carefully curated explanations and segues that help everyone to understand what is being done, but to aim it at a group other than the one actually at worship seems to me to lack integrity.

We can undermine our integrity very easily by poor reframing, by pretending to be people we are not, or by pretending we are interested in something we are not. We can do it unintentionally by not aligning our words and actions. In regular church life, the latter is perhaps the most common. We say that all are welcome, then make it clear that what you wear and how you talk or don't talk are important. We say that Jesus loves us all equally and we are of equal value, then choose just a few to lead the "special" parts of worship. We say that Jesus is inclusive, then limit participation in communion to the baptized.

Faye was a part of our church community and a school teacher in the government system. She felt God was calling her to teach in Afghanistan. The mission she was going with phoned our church to arrange a commissioning service for her where we would "set her aside" as a missionary, pray for her, and offer her our financial and prayer support. Of course, I agreed. Then I stopped and thought about what we would be saying to our community—the five other school teachers in particular. We would be saying, "You are all equal, but some are more equal than others." Years of talking would be undermined in a few minutes of action.

In the end, we went ahead with the commissioning, but we reframed the context. We made it clear that we were focusing on Faye and praying for her because:

1. She was going to Afghanistan where women are not treated well. She would be a Western woman in that context.
2. She was a single woman.
3. She was returning after several years back in New Zealand recovering from burnout and was unsure how she would cope.

We offered the community the chance to support Faye financially because, unlike the other teachers in our congregation, she wasn't going to be paid. We also recognized the other teachers there that morning and prayed for them.

This experience made me very aware of trying to keep our words aligned with our actions in worship and church life. It led to creating an annual list of all the vocations people were involved in, a list we included in our newsletter with the heading, "Pray for the ministries of our congregation."

Failure

This should be a well-worn word in your vocabulary. Dreaming big and aiming high (as you will be) dramatically increases the risk of failure. The more ideas you have, the more great ideas you will have, which means you'll have more ideas that don't pan out, or flop, or simply fail. But failure is not the end of the story. To many people, Jesus' death was the ultimate failure. Some of us know better.

German philosopher Rudolph Bahro famously said, "When the forms of an old culture are dying, the new culture is created by a few people who are not afraid to be insecure." Who better than the church to be at the forefront of such risky endeavors.

Questions

Asking questions is more valuable than answering them, if they are the right questions. I have referred to a number of important questions already. They don't always have to be answered fully or succinctly, but they must be asked and contemplated. It's often in the process of asking that the issues become clarified.

Don't be afraid to ask and not be able to answer, even during a worship event. My friend Christop tweets the questions he finds in the lectionary reading each week.[24] Not the questions Christop wants to ask of the text, but the questions the text itself states. Just reading those questions can be inspiring, encouraging, insightful, and challenging. Apparently Jesus was asked 180 questions in the gospels. He answered only three directly. I haven't counted.

5

A New Language for Worship: Describing Curation Practices

Once the bigger principles described in chapter 4 have been worked into your philosophy of curation, there are still many smaller but no less significant practices that need to be considered as you develop a new vocabulary and language. So now we look at some language that you might use around your practice of curation:

- reframing
- bundling and unbundling
- pace
- dark
- space
- juxtaposition
- liturgy
- preaching and Scripture
- evaluation
- silence and other spiritual practices
- songs
- candles
- incense
- segues
- takeaways/takeouts

REFRAMING

Reframing is a counseling term used in Neuro-Linguistic Programming. It relies on the idea that the meaning of an event, and our emotional response to it, depends on the context in which the event is perceived. A Chinese Taoist story about a farmer in a poor country village illustrates the process:

> He was considered very well-to-do because he owned a horse which he used for ploughing and for transportation. One day his horse ran away. All his neighbours exclaimed how terrible this was, but the farmer simply said, "Maybe." A few days later the horse returned and brought two wild horses with it. The neighbours all rejoiced at this good fortune, but the farmer just said "Maybe." The next day the farmer's son tried to ride one of the wild horses; the horse threw him and broke his leg. The neighbours all offered their sympathy for his misfortune, but the farmer again said, "Maybe." The next week conscription officers came to the village to take young men for the army. They rejected the farmer's son because of his broken leg. When the neighbours told him how lucky he was, the farmer replied, "Maybe."[25]

The meaning of a event can be changed if the event is given a different frame or context. Having two wild horses is a good thing until it's seen in the context of a broken leg. The broken leg seems like a bad thing in the context of peaceful village life, but it suddenly becomes good in the context of being conscripted to go to war.

Jokes and comedy also depend on reframing. Most jokes are based on a situation in which something we understand in one way takes on a different meaning or a variety of different meanings. It is given a new context. Les Barker, a British comedian from an earlier era, sings a very funny song called, "Have You Got Any News of the Iceberg?" about the sinking of the Titanic. The song is written from the perspective of the penguins on the iceberg that the Titanic hit. It is their cry to know what has happened to their friends who were on the iceberg—a nice piece of reframing.

In a worship context, reframing is about taking something from nonworship culture—a song, movie, saying, piece of art—and using it in worship. Reframing involves both context and content. Curators must have a full understanding of both in order to reframe cultural artifacts appropriately for worship.

The following story illustrates the dangers inherent in not being fully aware of the content you are reframing.

> The other day, I went to the local religious bookstore, where I saw a "Honk if you love Jesus" bumper sticker. I bought it and put it on the back bumper of my car, and I'm really glad I did. What an uplifting experience followed!

> I was stopped at the lights at a busy intersection, just lost in thought about the Lord, and didn't notice that the light had changed. That bumper sticker really worked! I found lots of people who love Jesus. Why, the guy behind me started to honk like crazy. He must really love the Lord, because pretty soon, he leaned out his window and yelled, "Jesus Christ!" as loud as he could. It was like a football game, with him shouting, "Go, Jesus Christ, go!" Everyone else started honking, too, so I leaned out my window

and waved and smiled at all of those Jesus-loving people.

There must have been some guy from Florida back there, because I could hear him yelling something about a "sunny beach," and saw him waving in a funny way with only his middle finger stuck up in the air. I asked my two kids what that meant. They kind of squirmed, looked at each other, giggled, and told me that it was the Florida good luck sign. So I leaned out the window and gave him the good luck sign back, God bless him.

Several cars behind, a very nice man stepped out of his car and yelled something. I couldn't hear him very well, but it sounded like, "Mother's father" or "Mother's from there." Maybe he was from Florida too. He must really love the Lord.

A couple of people were so caught up in the joy of the moment that they got out of their cars and were walking toward me. I bet they wanted to pray, but just then I noticed that the light was changing again, so I stepped on the gas. And a good thing I did, because I was the only driver to get across the intersection before the red.

I looked back at them standing there. I leaned way out the window, gave them a big smile, and held up the Florida good luck sign as I drove away.

Praise the Lord for such wonderful folks. [26]

Worship curating can involve taking artifacts—movies, music, incidents, rituals, objects—from the culture and from our everyday lives and using them in a worship context. Sometimes it involves taking biblical material and putting it into a twenty-first-century Western context. Jesus was the ultimate reframer, with the most obvious example being his reframing of bread and wine—common items at an ordinary meal—as mystical symbols of his body and blood. We, in turn, reframe Jesus' actions every time we curate the Lord's Supper.

Reframing is much more than simply using objects in a new way. As curators, we need to think through what each of the artifacts will signify and whether the reframing actually supports or undermines the shift we are seeking. I often use a large, black, plastic garbage can filled with water as a symbol for confession. I invite people to take a black stone, hold it in their hand, make their prayer, and then let the stone fall into the deep, black water. It disappears from sight.

I experienced a similar station as a worshiper in someone else's worship. We were told to pick up a stone and drop it into a bowl of water as a sign of God washing away our sins. However this bowl of water was white and shallow. The problem was that the water was just washing my sins! I could see the colored stones—my "sins"—sparkling clean and sitting on the bottom of the bowl staring back at me. This disconnect may have been the result of the curator not testing the props first, of not giving sufficient thought to what she wanted to say, or simply of a lack of experience. Whatever the reason, it was a jarring experience.

Hymns can be particularly dissonant. Their language and imagery can not only ring false—Christmas songs about snow, winter, and blustery this and that don't work very well in the heat of midsummer Christmas in Australia—but become distracting. I usually try to find versions of hymns that are gender friendly and free of *thee*s and *thou*s.

If I can't find them, I make my own changes where possible. If Old English or patriarchal language can't be changed, I will make some introductory comments such as, "This is an old hymn that has some language and ideas in it we wouldn't normally use today, but it is a hymn that has a lot of meaning for some of our community, and it's one that connects us with those who have gone before us in the faith." The introduction provides a new frame or context.

Ash Wednesday is the first day of the Lenten season and often involves marking the forehead with a cross drawn with ash. This ash is traditionally made up of the burned palms saved from the previous year's Palm Sunday. Working with a community where we didn't expect people to turn out on any day other than Sunday, we usually ended up celebrating Ash Wednesday on the first Sunday of Lent using potting mix and fragrant oil—and a good deal of explanation. Reframing.

At SEEDS church in Melbourne, we always used refreshing iced water in medium-sized glass tumblers for communion. We explained that some members of our community needed to stay away from alcohol. We didn't like the traditional Baptist grape juice, and we didn't want to create a two-tier system of alcohol and juice. Water, which carries significant symbolism for the church and for Australians through the early exploration of Australia and the explorers' relationships with Aboriginal people, seemed a suitable replacement. This was a highly contextualized reframing that worked very well.

One evening, a young man who had recently arrived from Bangalore approached me following the service and explained that for him water meant open sewers that were definitely not drinkable or refreshing. The water was a stumbling block for his participation in the communion. That is the risk with reframing, but the risk is no greater than the reading of any biblical story with its unfamiliar cultural setting.

Using the ancient form of Stations of the Cross in a contemporary setting is an increasingly common form of reframing. The degree of reframing varies, from those who retain the traditional form but place it in a new context to those who use large-scale installations of contemporary art to tell the same story.

Using contemporary music tracks, movie clips, or ideas from installation art in worship calls for careful reframing. Good reframing requires us to understand the essence of the truth we're connecting with and the significance of the artifact or event we're transferring into the worship event. Surface connections between the two events or symbols are not enough. We also have to know the people for whom we are reframing. What is their context? What assumptions and ideas will they bring with them? Finally, we must have a solid sense of church history and tradition. If we're going to reframe an age-old ritual, we need to know its origins and respect its history. Reframing is a task fraught with potential pitfalls but an essential one if we are to connect the gospel with the everyday lives of people inside and outside the church.

BUNDLING AND UNBUNDLING

Bundling is a marketing term that describes the packaging of several items together as one unit, for example, shampoo and conditioner. You have to buy both even if you only want one, or to get the cheaper item you have to also buy the more expensive one. The computer industry uses it a lot, particularly with software where numerous applications are bundled together and supplied with your computer.

This has several implications for church and worship life. We bundle churches, so we know what to expect of them and in them. We know seeker-driven churches will have contemporary music, casually dressed pastors, and childcare. The Pentecostals will have a lot of singing, a long sermon, and the whole event will be loud and music driven. If we are going to create new ways of operating missionally in the settings we are in, we have to unbundle all of that and more.

Unbundling could refer to your church and its relationship to the ethos of the denomination you are part of. Maybe it would benefit from adding some of the ingredients of other denominational bundles and dropping some of its own. It's a great pity that we mostly leave the work of the Holy Spirit to the Pentecostals, social justice to the Mennonites, and ritual to the Catholics.

We also need to unbundle what we do in worship and offer it in smaller/slower portions. We don't need to cover the whole gospel every time we meet, cater to all desires, all ages and stages, all intelligences in every worship event. We can offer a range over time. But we do need to be fully aware of the range of stages that people are at, especially stages of spiritual formation. We seem to expect that different churches will cater to different stages of faith. Why can't the worship and programs of a single church (or a small geographically close bundle of churches) be able to hold people through all ages and stages?

Unbundling involves asking hard questions about everything from the lighting, to the seating, to the timing of a worship event. Why do we sit and stand when we do? Why does the singing fall at this point and not at another? What would change if we gathered on a different day or at a different time? Questions like these will lead you to new places of discovery and build your curation skill set.

PACE

After three days of standing in front of the hyperslow-motion videos of Bill Viola's *The Passions* in Canberra in 2005 (not continuously!), I was left wondering what these videos had to say about the slow-worship concept and what they might mean for worship I curated. These works by Viola move excrutiatingly slowly—so slow that unless you stand still and focus consistently, you are unaware that they are not stills. The easiest way to be aware of their movement is to go away for five minutes and return. You miss the unfolding, but become convinced that there is movement. I was surprised at the large number of people who would stand in front of one of the huge screens for twenty seconds, apparently see nothing, and move on. This was, after all, advertised as a video installation.

If you don't slow down, you don't see it.

Artist Anthony McCall says he wants his light-line sculptural works to move more slowly than the people observing them. In other words, the fastest objects in the room should be the people. There is something in that for the worship we curate. There is a time for a faster pace, and there is a time (perhaps more often) for a slower one. Pace is not just about speed. It's also about the segues that connect elements in our worship and ensuring people have enough time to engage and disengage with one element before moving on to the other. A good call to worship eases people from life at one pace to that at another. What is expected when people come into the worship space also affects this segue. Do they come in talking or silent?

DARK

Reducing the light levels helps the brain disengage from the cacophony of messages assaulting the body and its senses. It creates a more womb-like experience and allows people to better absorb what is coming through their ears. Worship often takes place in daylight, but when it doesn't, consider what you can do with various light levels. Altering light levels can signal a segue, in the same way changing music can. But be aware that darkness has different connotations for different people. Don't assume it feels safe for everyone.

SPACE

Otherwise known as "the room" or the physical context in which the worship event takes place, the space in which you find yourself will always play a significant role in worship.

Most of us have to work with what we have. Rows of fixed seats aren't easy to shift, and the rupture that doing so would cause to the community isn't worth it. But there are ways to introduce movement if you are creative and patient.

I once curated only the sermon in a very tightly-pewed Baptist building with an equally conservative congregation. I finished the sermon by asking people to take the two small squares of paper— one blue and one green—I had included with the bulletin. I had them start by holding the blue one and praying in silence for someone or some situation that needed an influx of hope. (The sermon had been on hope.) After a minute or so, I asked them to take the green piece in their hand and pray for a situation or area of their own lives in which they needed God to enter and bring hope. Then I prayed for us all. People were encouraged to put the two papers on their fridge or bathroom mirror to remind them of their prayers that morning. More than a year later a woman in her nineties told me she still had the papers on her fridge and still used them to pray. Work with what you have.

Good space and seating arrangements alone don't guarantee strong worship, community, or participation. So while the space needs careful consideration and is definitely a significant part of the curator's responsibility, it doesn't have to dictate what the worship will look like. It's a factor to include in the mix.

Where the elements of the curation take place in the space, however, does shape the worship event and so demands very careful analysis in advance. Where readers' voices come from, where images are projected, where communion is served, and what is considered the "front," all affect the strength of the worship. I like projections to come as far around the sides, if not to the back, of the room as possible so that people shift their gaze and move their bodies to look at them even if they are seated in rows.[26] If I had my way, all musicians would be at least to the side of the platform and ideally on the seating level as well. They need to be heard, not seen center stage. I want the front-center space to be for the rituals and corporate responses of the worship.

A curated space is one in which every aspect of the space has been considered and taken into account. The space is the context into which the content will be placed, presented, performed, or further curated. Spaces should change according to the content. At World Vision staff chapel services during Advent, I move all the seating from being in rows to being in a U formation. It says something different is going on. I did the same for a recent memorial service. It says to the community, "Today is a bit different from other days in this space." At Easter, the color of the fabric on the cross or altar (read "table" in my settings) is different than that at Pentecost or during Ordinary Time.

JUXTAPOSITION

Elements don't always have to flow seamlessly or be obviously connected. Contrasts can be good. They make you think. I still remember seeing a sign on a Catholic school that read, "Irish Pub Night," then on the next line, "March 8, Stations of the Cross." Humor in a seemingly inappropriate place might also work well. A physical setting may be juxtaposed with the content that is put in it. This is most often done accidentally and with unhelpful effect.

I have experienced loud, recorded music played in what had been a quiet reflective worship event. The dominance of the particular lyrics in the track, compared to what preceded and followed, somehow made the track work. Think about how both the content and context of the elements and artifacts of your worship event will sit with each other.

LITURGY

While some of you will have a comfortable relationship with this word, many will not. You need to get friendly with it. Curators design liturgy and then help their communities engage with God through that liturgy.

The term comes from the Greek *leitourgia* and means "the work of the people," "public work," or "duty." *Liturgy* is the work we all do when we come to worship. So despite what some churches would say strongly—even vehemently—to the contrary, every church worship event, from the wildest Pentecostal to the most sedate Friends service is liturgy. It is the structure, the pattern, the form that is followed by people at worship. If you want to argue that in your church it's actually only the worship leader, band, and preacher who are doing any work, then I'll accept that perhaps you don't have any liturgy. But you probably won't have any corporate worship either, just a concert.

Let's bring back the term in its rightful place and use.

PREACHING AND SCRIPTURE

These are familiar terms that I want to explore briefly in the light of what I am proposing about worship. I'm not in the school that wants to dismiss the spoken word or even the solo spoken sermon as no longer having any value in worship. The question isn't whether or not preaching works today or even about what preaching might look like in a postmodern context. The question should always be about the ways we can best sustain the people of our communities in their following of Christ in the world. What resources do we need to ensure they are being sustained and what's the best way to ensure they keep on that journey?

If you decide preaching is one of those ways, then I do think the long and academic monologue is past its expiration date. But there is a place for carefully and thoughtfully crafted sermons that connect the biblical story with the lives of the community at worship. The same rules I have previously suggested apply to other elements of worship also apply to the sermon. While I think preaching can be significant in shaping and moving a congregation, I don't see the sermon as pivotal or of primary significance in a worship event. If the goal of our worship is to have people encounter and engage with the Trinitarian community of God, and we see the biblical text as foundational to that engagement (as I do), there are many ways to enable that. Preaching in the traditional sense is just one of them. *Lectio divina* and a slew of ancient ways of engaging with the Bible are readily available today. One of my friends says, "If you read the gospels without getting hungry you aren't really paying attention." Preaching needs to make people hungry for Jesus, justice, and transformation. It works best in the context of a well-curated worship event.

If you insist on using the monologue, you can follow it up with a set of stations that give pace, space, and time for people to soak in the story. You can find a piece of art that shows an interpretation of, and response to, the story about which you are preaching. Let the congregation engage with this as a group, and you will find the comments being made are often more insightful than the ones you make. Not knowing much about art, I devised the following standard set of questions to ask about any piece of art I use in relation to a biblical text:

- What stands out to you from this painting?
- What part or parts of the story has the artist chosen to depict here?
- What moment in the story has been captured?
- Why do you think he chose that?
- What was the artist wanting the people of his or her day to understand about the story?
- If you were the artist, what moment in the story would you want to capture?
- Why that part?

Sometimes a Google search of the artist will produce some interesting material to feed into the conversation.

Here's another example of how to preach without preaching. Having read Walter Brueggemann's wonderful *Message of the Psalms*, I wanted to introduce my community to some of his insights. Rather than preach a monologue, I gave out sheets with three psalms on them (13, 30, and 33). We read them through twice out loud, and people were asked to select the one that spoke to them most. They were then handed a sheet relating to that psalm. What they didn't know at the time was that each psalm came under a different one of the three categories Brueggemann describes for psalms: orientation, disorientation, and new orientation. So they were likely to have chosen a psalm that reflected where they were in life at that time. In addition to a brief written introduction to the particular psalm and what Brueggemann says about it, each sheet carried the same suggestions for reflection and response:

1. Does this resonate with you? Are you aware of anything going on in your life at present that suggests this is true for you? What drew you to this psalm? List those things here:

   When you have made your list, go to the incense station and burn several grains of incense as a symbol of your praise and gratitude to God for being present with you in your current circumstances.

2. Are there aspects of your life and living that you want to talk with God about? Perhaps other people or situations to pray for? List those things here:

   When you have made your list, go to the candle-lighting station and light a candle as a symbol of your prayer for those situations.

3. Bruggemann suggests that the life of a follower of Jesus consists of two decisive moves that are always underway. He says we are regularly surprised by and regularly resist these moves. One is the move out of a settled orientation into a sense of disorientation. This may be slow, abrupt, feel unsafe, feel exciting, threaten to dismantle what we believe and feel to be true. It may come from circumstances beyond, or within, our control.

> The other move is from a context of disorientation to a new orientation. This may feel safe, settled, stable, bring relief, or have the opposite effect if something within us would prefer to stay in a state of disorientation. We may learn something about God, our relationship with God, about ourself, or we may not.
>
> Do you sense either of these moves being underway in your life at present? How do you feel about that? Is God saying something to you about your current situation, the one you are moving toward, or the transition from one to another?
>
> When you have reflected on this, return to either the incense or the candle-lighting station and make your prayer or your praise.

In this way, we were able to offer quite specific applications of a large block of Scripture to each person without having to broadcast the message to the whole congregation.

Often I will read a large chunk of the Bible as part of a worship event, regardless of whether it is being preached from or providing the context for stations. I do this particularly at times like Easter and Christmas, so people get more of an understanding of the story's flow and context rather than just isolated texts.

EVALUATION

You should evaluate every worship event you curate. I don't need to tell you to evaluate other worship events you participate in because once you've been curating for a while, you won't be able to stop yourself doing that. Preferably evaluate in conversation with someone you trust to give you honest feedback. Try to write down your evaluations. Be specific rather than general and vague. Measure against the values you hold as a church and your understanding of what you want to achieve through worship: What did you want to say? Don't project your own preferences onto everyone. You may not like opera music, but maybe in the context it worked well. I will discuss in more detail how to evaluate worship in chapter 7.

SILENCE AND OTHER SPIRITUAL PRACTICES

I find it desperately sad and of great concern that the Christian church in the West has given away its heritage of spiritual practices at a time in history when the desire for them from unchurched people is at a new height. *Ecce Homo,* "Behold the Man," an exhibition of paintings of Jesus Christ, was the most visited exhibition the National Gallery of England has ever mounted. The 2006 United Kingdom reality television series, *The Monastery,* where young men submitted themselves to monastery life for forty days and nights, was a phenomenal success. The follow-up book, *Finding Sanctuary: Monastic Steps for Everyday Life,* by Abbot Christopher Jamison sold out of three printings. Philip Groning spent several years inside the Mother House of the Carthusian Order of Monks filming the rhythm of silence and repetition. The resulting movie, *Into Great Silence,* which featured the monks without commentary or backing music, was released worldwide. I appreciate that in the church in the West there are pockets of renewed interest in spiritual disciplines and rhythms of life that sustain spirituality in the daily barrage of pressures that is contemporary life, but the outsider would be hard-pressed to access them. Why is it that people are more likely to seek out a form of Buddhism than a Christian community when they want to learn to meditate, to look to Islam when they want to learn to pray? Why can silence so rarely be found in a service of worship beyond the Friends?

Under the heading, "Silent Night, Party Night," *The Weekend Australian* reported:

> Beijing, New York, and Washington cottoned on to a new way to "lessen the overall volume of modern life," namely the "Quiet Party," invented in the Big Apple. *The Washington Post* reported that for about $12, patrons could attend a dimly lit venue with no music and communicate by scribbling on index cards which they handed to each other. Alcohol was permitted and apart from passing notes, participants could play Scrabble, chess, and draughts. If or when the silence became too much they could seek the "low volume" area and talk quietly. "You have to rely on a pen and paper and your personality" one man said. "It takes the non-essential stuff and strips it out."[28]

Into Great Silence features a scene in which two monks are handsawing logs for firewood. The older monk has an easy, fluid, unhurried style. Cutting the wood seems effortless. The new monk is hurried and harried. He saws faster, his movements are jerky, and he breaks out in a sweat. He makes the job seem difficult. Our outer world reflects our inner one. The way we live is driven by who we are and what we believe. To teach our communities about creation care is pointless unless we have first enabled them to confront their greed. Spiritual disciplines can help resolve this tension.

I realize that it isn't possible to teach and to model in every service everything needful for following Jesus. But surely, over time, we should be able to offer people a range of possibilities for sustaining and challenging their interior lives, drawn from the traditions of the church. Sustaining people in their following of Christ in the world isn't a one-size-fits-all deal. Different personalities and learning styles demand that the worship curator and the preacher understand the possibilities and make them available over time to the worshiping community. Silence and a variety of spiritual practices need to be taught, modeled, and supported by worship.

Silence is worth thinking about in both the aural and visual senses. The most famous work of aural silence is probably American composer John Cage's 4' 33", pronounced "4 minutes, 33 seconds" (Cage called it "4, 33"). It is in three movements that are often wrongly described as silence when they in fact carry the ambient background sounds of the musicians sitting waiting to play for the duration of each movement. Cage wanted us to think of any sound as music. The piece is a reminder that less can be more. Silence is essential if we want to slow worship down.

Visual silence may be even more important than aural silence when it comes to worship. A movie consists of a long strip of images separated by a thin black line—a visual silence. Without this visual silence, the movie would be a blur of fuzzy images without clear movement or story. I have heard of churches that don't use any environmental projections during Lent in order to have the community focus on the season and its story. They bring them back on Easter Sunday. That's a very nice modern reframing of the traditional stripping the church building of all color and ornamentation that many liturgical churches do during Lent.

The poet Rilke once described music as "the rest between the notes." Without silence—aurally and visually—life is reduced to less than what God intended it to be.

St. Benedict uses two words to describe silence: *quies* and *silentium*. *Quies* is the silence of the absence of noise. It is valuable for people with busy urban lives. *Silentium* is an attitude of attentiveness toward God. It is the silence of paying loving attention. We have a responsibility to ensure the worship we curate brings healing and clarity rather than encouraging rupture and confusion. Silence of both sorts in appropriate places is an important part of that.

The dictum, "Do not speak unless it improves on the silence," is a useful guide for worship curators, and the best silence is that found when a worship event finishes early.

SONGS

This is hardly new vocabulary, but I would like to try to give it some new content. We take for granted that singing will be part of worship. Yet church services, and perhaps Welsh rugby games, are the only places in our culture where we are expected to sing regardless of our ability. I don't like singing. I like standing among people who sing well, but I don't sing well myself. Most of the worship I curate and lead doesn't include a block of singing. I'm not capable of leading it. I might include a hymn, a Taizé chant, or another short song, and if I do, they are usually sung a cappella. Since I don't sing well, they need to be well-known songs that others can pick up quickly. In regular services where musicians are supplied, I let others choose the songs and lead the singing, although I might choose a hymn or song as part of the response time.

The question of congregational singing is a conflicted one. How much singing is too much or too little? Some people may have come to your church to get away from endlessly repeated choruses and emotional manipulation through music. They would be quite happy never to sing in church again. But for others, group singing is an important mode of expression and creates an environment where they can respond to God most deeply and effectively. There is the further difficulty of the limited availability of songs in which the lyrics and images are relevant to our lived experience, and that manage to avoid the jargon, shallow theology, sexist language, and archaisms of much worship music.

The positive side of singing is that it's a corporate, participatory, physical event. Over time, people learn songs they can use in private devotions and other situations where they may be together with others from their community. When I worked with Urban Seed in Melbourne, there were a large number of songs that everyone knew and could sing a capella in any situation. These songs were often written by past and present community members and reflected some aspect of Urban Seed's journey. Singing them was a very significant community-building tool.

Congregational singing is, as Ruth Duck describes it, "inherently collective" and can be a form by which the community can express faith together.[29] This is particularly valuable in the absence of more formal creeds. This makes it all the more important that the music and lyrics actually express faith in a way that can be recognized and affirmed by the congregation. A service should rarely pass without any music at all, but this may well be recorded rather than live, secular rather than sacred.

I dislike singing, but I love music. So I usually include a recorded song in the worship events I curate. It may be a song that sets the theme, is part of the response, or runs behind an element of the service. I have the lyrics available either in a handout, data projection, or both. It is arrogant to assume that everyone will know the track well enough to know the words and especially that they will be able to reflect on those lyrics without having them available. There is no point in playing a track if people have little idea of what the song is about. The only exception to this would be if the song was being used more for mood or had only a repeated line or two that I wanted the congregation to "hear."

I try to use tracks that don't require any introduction or background in order to understand them. One favorite is "The Wood Song" by the Indigo Girls.[30] It's a great song, but I tend to focus on the refrain when I use it. Speaking of a boat that is barely able to carry its load, they sing, "but the wood is tired and the wood is old and we'll make it fine if the weather holds. But if the weather holds then we'll have missed the point." I use this with a focus on those lines, so I mention them in introduction and include them highlighted among the rest of the lyrics.

I rarely use tracks from the Christian-music industry. A recorded song from the wider culture is a more useful way of connecting the everyday lives of the community to their worship and spirituality. Some of these may well be performed by artists who are Christian. Obvious examples would be songs by U2 such as "Yahweh," "40," and "Wake Up Dead Man."

Among groups at worship around the world are several who have taken the principles of community participation and interactivity very seriously in relation to songs, singing, and music. Todd and Angie Fadel at The Bridge in Portland, Oregon, developed a process they call "The Whirrship." Todd recently described their worship in an e-mail to me as, "Anthems. Shouted anthems. Spirituals. Punk spirituals. Garage gospel. Passion before precision. Female-fronted. I play the piano like Jerry Lee Lewis, so female-fronted, boogie woogie garage gospel. Garage spirituals."[31] But that hardly explains their process or what it is like to be part of it. Todd explains further:

> We believe that every community has their own voice
> . . . . Our passion is to help them figure out what their
> songs are for their community. . . . A songwriting
> game for example. If you put anything in the context
> of a game, it tricks our minds into feeling that things

are approachable and manageable. What we do, we start covertly helping people develop this ability to not be critical of each other's expression. We involve every age group and background.

I see it as a community being like a 50-legged race. You know the 3-legged race where you're tied together? Everyone has one leg tied together. At the beginning, it's the most awkward, gross feeling and you don't know what to do but then after a while, you just count, 1-2, 1-2 and soon, you have this community, 50 people strong walking, slowly but surely to a goal. That's possible with any community. . . .

So we'll play games and help people develop tools of being non-critical, helping people to look at one another in a loving, inclusive way, laying their aesthetics and preferences aside in hopes of making a beautiful collage.[32]

Admittedly, The Bridge is not your average church. Their community is made up of people who would not generally find a place in churches. (House rules for church services used to include: all dogs must be on a leash, no snakes near the food table, bathing suit areas of the body must be covered. Rules that apparently needed regular enforcing!)

Tribe, a church in Los Angeles, makes community drumming—with chants, speaking, and songs over parts of it—a significant part of their worship. At a worship event I attended, the call to worship was the sound of a solo drum from the room adjoining the one where we had eaten together. It set a rhythm picked up by all other worshipers using their own or supplied percussion instruments. We passed through a curtain of various sheer and net fabrics into the worship space where David Raven was sitting on a drum stool inserted in the circle of chairs. He was playing a hand drum and a foot-pedal bass drum, while also modulating a chord via a synthesizer and mixer. The electronica exited through two large speaker bins, covered with cloth, placed in the center of the room, altar-like. Several candles sat on top forming a centerpiece.

In my journal I wrote:

> People find a seat in the circle and join in, following or rising over David's lead. After three or four minutes he begins singing a short and simple song over the heavy drumming. Words go up on the screen (the screen is split in half by hanging net fabric. These varying widths and four layers produce an almost 3-D effect on the icon projected on the left side. The right side is left clear as text can't be read through the layers. Rebecca leads an opening prayer. We "sing" two more songs and play one instrumental piece. The drumming rises to a crescendo and falls according to our communal and unspoken will. David is a professional drummer and very skilled at what he does with us. It's a thunderous sound at times. I love it.

Psalms, hymns, and spiritual songs can take many forms.

CANDLES

I wouldn't usually include any specific reference to candles as most people take them for granted as the stock-in-trade of a worship curator, but I have had a significant number of people ask why I use candles in worship and what they mean. It's unfortunate that new forms of worship are so often associated with using candles, as if the "if-we-light-it-they-will-come" mantra actually works.

My first experience of being questioned about candles was after curating a very brief piece of worship to illustrate the principles I had talked about in a short seminar with a group of leaders from a Pentecostal church. Two middle-aged men expressed their anger at the offense I had caused them by having two large candles burning during the worship. They claimed that candles were satanic and had no place in Christian worship or a Christian place of worship. I wondered out loud if their response was a reaction against their previous involvement with the occult and, when asked, they exploded with even greater rage at such a suggestion. They clearly had no knowledge of church history.

Christop Booth does hospitality with marginalized people in downtown Melbourne and says this about their use of candles in worship:

> During our prayer times, before lunch in Credo Café, we often light candles as symbols of our prayer. This might seem strange for a community that was started by Baptists (Baptists traditionally prefer words rather than visuals). One of the reasons we use candles is that they help us to see. The first candle we light symbolises Christ. We believe that it is Christ who helps us to see what is really going on in our world—like the light of a candle. All the other candles are lit from the Christ-candle. Another reason we use candles is that it means we don't have to be able to construct eloquent, articulate [verbal] prayers. While it's nice to be able to say beautiful prayers, for many of us who gather to pray in Credo, the sense that our prayers need to sound nice can make it difficult to pray at all.

By choosing to express our prayers through an action that almost anyone can do, we can take the emphasis off having to be able to speak nicely.[33]

The most common form of candle lighting will be that using the small individual candles known as votives. Votive offerings, votive candles, votive masses are very much a Catholic thing. The name itself comes from the Latin word *votivus*, from *votum* meaning "a vow" or "a promise."

As my Catholic priest friend says, "To be a little cynical, [vows] were a bit like futures-dealing with Jesus, Mary, and Joseph and all the holy saints of heaven." The promise symbolized by the votive candle has a long tradition in Catholic practice but was particularly popular around the time of the Crusades. It went a bit like this: "God, You get me home from this mess, and I will build a chapel/church/basilica in your honor." Less spectacular "votives" are made today. Lighting a votive candle can be a symbol of our prayer or of our promise to God. A candle tray can be made available in pretty much any worship event or sacred space. It doesn't have to be a specified station. It can sit unobtrusively at the side with a sign that simply says, "Light a candle at any time as a symbol of your prayer for. . . ."

I prefer votive candles over heating candles as they look better and take up less room in a sand tray. I will never extinguish a candle or tray of candles while the worshiping community is present. If I can't leave them to safely burn out, I wait until people have left before blowing them out. Children need to be trained to not build bonfires with candles left burning or to feed them with spare paper bulletins. Similarly I don't like to reuse prayer candles, but I can see how a connection could be made with the prayers of others by doing so.

A paper bag with sand in the bottom makes an excellent light source that doesn't blow out in the wind. Make sure the sides of the bag are well away from the candle flame. Video loops of candles burning also work well in the right setting, especially if they run on a collection of television sets around the space. A live video feed of a candle tray as more and more people light candles through a worship event looks stunning.[34]

INCENSE

The sense of smell is often neglected in worship. But having a bowl of glowing charcoal that people can drop a grain of incense into as a symbol of their prayer or commitment is a beautiful multisensory experience. Too much incense, however, is an asthmatic's nightmare. There are some techniques to getting the process working properly, so ask your local Catholic or Episcopalian priest for a lesson and where to source the incense and charcoal.

I often run a video loop of an Eastern Orthodox thurifer (swinger) swinging a thurible (burning charcoal and incense container on chains) behind the bowl of charcoal.[35] Alongside it will be the text of Psalm 141:1, 2 or Revelation 8:4, which connect incense with prayer. For a Baptist, incense is a wonderful novelty. For some in your community, it may revive memories of difficult church experiences. All the previously raised questions apply.

SEGUES

The pronunciation of this term varies from "segways" to "seegs." The former Americanization seems to be taking over despite the Italian origins of the word. It means "to follow." Regardless of how you pronounce it, segues are the links that connect one element in worship to the next. They are vital and generally fall to the curator, unless the worship flow has been very well prepared and the participants are confident and aware of the overall flow. Segues can include silence, explanations, and playing a piece of music. Within a worship event, there need to be clear instructions for each element as well as a way to opt out of any involvement. This happens in the segues.

They also apply to physical movement and include entering and transitioning spaces. Getting from the parking lot into the worship space is a segue. Even in very familiar spaces and after many years of curating worship, I often walk through the running order in advance, in the space, and imagine what it will be like for people to follow and participate in the worship, and where the props of the service need to be at particular times. Segues determine pace and flow.

TAKEAWAYS/TAKEOUTS

I try to have something physical that people can take away from each worship event, or even element, I curate. This might be as simple as a piece of paper that lists the stations, the words of a key song, or a printout of the biblical text from the event. Or it might be more substantial like a small barbed-wire cross, a piece of string, or a shell. These enable the encounter that began in the worship event to be continued over days, months, and even years. I have a collection of miscellaneous objects acquired in this way. I still remember why I have them. When I can't remember the story of a particular piece, I throw it out. I've had one piece for thirty years.

CONCLUSION

There are many more terms that we could define and connect to the practice of curating worship. Even the terms I have described could be greatly expanded. My hope is that by giving you a small insight into the ways a broader vocabulary and language can be used when designing and curating worship, you will start to see this practice as significantly deeper and more important than just organizing a service. With that foundation, we will move on to the impact the curation model can have on the building and strengthening of the community for whom the worship is curated.

6

A New Language for Worship: Building Community through Curation

O nce you begin to apply some of the principles and processes described so far, you will discover that there are positive changes happening in the lives of individuals and groups within your community that you hadn't anticipated. This final collection of new vocabulary and language includes ways of working that have the benefit of enabling deeper engagement with worship, God, and each other:

- collaboration
- transformation
- liminality
- communitas
- community
- hospitality
- depth and breadth
- interactivity
- terms that shouldn't be in the worship curator's vocabulary

COLLABORATION

Collaboration is about working together to plan and design as well as curate worship events. It's not easy to do well. A group process has the significant advantage of stimulating greater creativity and ownership and of bringing out the best in all involved. The downside is that it takes much longer than going through the process alone, requires many meetings, and can result in a mediocre outcome in order to satisfy everyone involved. And sometimes dealing with the group dynamics takes up more time and energy than the worship planning.

In my experience, collaborative planning works best when people are brought together because of the specific skills or abilities they have to contribute to the process. On one occasion, I deliberately set out to find someone who was good with language and story, another who was tech savvy, one who had a good visual sense for space and color, and one who knew music. This mix meant that when we met, each person had a specific perspective from which to contribute. There was no competition for acceptance of an idea as we tended to trust what each was bringing.

The musician and producer Brian Eno, in talking about how he works on collaborative music projects, says:

> Usually what people are practicing is not democracy but cowardice and good manners. Nobody wants to step on so-and-so's toes, so nobody wants to say anything. The valuable idea of democracy is that if there are five people in a room and one of them feels strongly about something, you can trust that the strength of their feelings indicates that there is something behind it. My feeling about a good democratic relationship is the notion that it's a

shifting leadership. It's not, "We all lead together all the time." It's, "We all have sufficient trust in one another to believe that if someone feels strongly then we will let them lead for that period of time."[36]

Collaborative curating is quite difficult and requires a high level of trust and confidence between the cocurators. It is a wonderful experience to work collaboratively with someone in whom you have complete confidence and with whom there is no sense of competition or ego boosting. The curator, whether alone or with another, can operate in a variety of ways—working with a team from start to finish, calling on others to produce the event when it has been designed, or as a solo creator-curator. Each can be appropriate in different settings. To have no outside participation or collaboration in the process is counterproductive and undermines the values I am proposing. A consistently solo curator runs the risk of becoming like a solo worship leader and mentors no successors. Collaboration is not about power or control and requires a reasonable level of maturity on the part of those collaborating.

Of course, there is a tension between those with experience and those new to the task. The more experience you have as a curator, the more difficult it becomes to work with those who lack it. You find you can work faster and more efficiently on your own. If you are able to work collaboratively as often as possible, you will find that others quickly learn what works and what doesn't, and the quality and value of their contribution to both planning and curation rises rapidly.

TRANSFORMATION

The transformation of people's lives must be the ultimate goal of worship, as it is for church life generally. I know all the arguments for worship being about glorifying God (whatever that might mean) and for worship to be God-centered. I just don't accept them as the end of the discussion. We are bodies and minds as well as spirits and souls. We follow Jesus in the context of a physical world. If our worship and church life don't constantly move us toward becoming more and more Christlike in how we shop and talk and make love, it has failed, regardless of how God-focused we claim it to be.

A life of words and actions and thoughts that are being transformed is more likely to bring glory to God than the endless singing of love songs to Jesus that bring no transformation. Transformation of the worshipers is the goal of all worship. This is an aspect of sustaining the people in our communities. It doesn't happen all at once but over time. But transformation is a work of the Holy Spirit, not of the curator. All we can do is work with the Spirit and offer to God what we do. But we can keep transformation in mind when we shape up the questions or content we use and the ways in which we encourage people to respond. This connects back to the open-endedness I talked about earlier. It's not my role as curator to decide how the Spirit of God will work transformatively in a person's life. My role is to provide space and place where that could happen. Don't be fooled into thinking that information leads to transformation. It rarely does.

If pressed, I would say that rather than focusing on transformation, the curator is better occupied thinking about crucifixion, crisis, and despair. There can be no resurrection (transformation) without crucifixion (deaths of one sort and size or another that generally come out of periods of crisis or despair) and only at the point of crucifixion can grace kick in and do her thing on behalf of God. Even the most dramatic of transformations is just the first step on a lifetime journey of transformations that will still not be complete at the end of a life on this earth. A good worship curator will always be aware of that and provide opportunities for those ongoing transformations and glimpses of God's grace to take place.

Allow space and time for the celebration of how far people have come and of how God has changed them, but also remind your community of how far there is to go. Focus on Jesus the Transformer rather than on one of those being transformed. We need to allow space for those in our worship who are like Tony Manero in the movie *Saturday Night Fever* when he said, "Sometimes you look at a crucifix and all you see is a man on a cross."

One of the temptations for any church or movement within the church is to seek change only when life is going badly—which in the church usually means when numbers are declining. Transformation—of individuals or communities—won't come about by repackaging church to make it more attractive or more relevant.

At a contemporary Stations of the Cross installation in Auckland, a young theological student encountered God in a transformative way. Fourteen pieces of art depicting fourteen moments in the last week of Jesus' life were installed around the outer walls of a large room. The walls had been covered with black fabric. At one point, the fabric covered an exit door so a sign that said "EMERGENCY EXIT" had been placed beside a slit in the fabric. It was this sign that God used to speak so clearly to this man. He later wrote to me, "I got halfway around the stations and I saw the emergency exit sign; I realised then that Jesus could have got out of his situation at any time, but he chose to stay to the end." It wasn't the art or the story that God spoke through, it was the sign. I could not have planned or engineered that response. Transformation comes through open-endedness. You can't curate transformation, but you can curate spaces in which it might happen.

LIMINALITY

During the 1960s, Scottish-American cultural anthropologist Victor Turner, working with his wife Edith, took a term from Arnold van Gennep's turn-of-the-century work *Rites of Passage* and applied it to a broader range of social situations. The term was *liminal,* from the Latin *limen* meaning "a threshold." Van Gennep isolated and named rites of passage as a category of the rituals common to all societies everywhere. These transitional rituals involve movement from separation, to margin, and through to reaggregation. The Turners wrote, "The first phase detaches the ritual subject from their old places in society; the last installs them, inwardly transformed and outwardly changed, in a new place in society."[37] The phase between the two, the time on the margins, is what Turner describes as the liminal phase or the period of experiencing liminality.

Van Gennep used the term to describe the process of young males in central African tribal societies moving from adolescence to adulthood. This involves the young boy being sent into the countryside alone to fend for himself (separation) and emerging some days later as a recognized and accepted full-fledged, sexually-active adult in the society (reaggregation). Temporary marginalization leads to an irreversible change in the participant's role and place in the society. Once transition has occurred, there is no going back to the original condition.

The Turners transferred this understanding to a much broader range of situations, particularly religious ones, and described in detail what is experienced during the transitional or liminal stage—the midtransition—in a rite of passage. Victor Turner wrote, "Liminal entities are neither here nor there; they are betwixt and between the positions assigned and arrayed by law, custom, convention, and ceremonial."[38]

The institutions, roles, and status that society grants us define and describe our lives. These structures of society shape who we become. From birth, they influence our identity and determine how we act in everyday life. But there is a dimension of life that falls outside these structures or, more specifically, between them or in their margins. This experience may have been entered upon voluntarily or thrust upon a person by a crisis of some sort. To be made redundant from your job would be an example of falling into this dimension. The social structures of having a job, going to the workplace, being defined by what you do, receiving regular income, having conversations about your work, are all removed. You are hopeful for another job but have not yet entered into that phase. You are between jobs and between the structures, the constructs, of society. You have left behind what previously defined your life, but you haven't yet moved forward. To be in the gaps between these structures is to be in a liminal existence, living on the margins, on the threshold. The Turners describe this as "anti-structure," that is, between the structures.[39]

Turner believed that the liminal phase was of crucial importance in the ritual process and explored it more seriously than other anthropologists of his day. To be in a liminal state is to be liberated in a way that may be experienced either positively or negatively. It is a no-man's-land experience. The person has moved beyond what has gone before, but has not yet fully arrived at what is ahead. Turner expanded the understanding of liminality to include almost any experience that temporarily suspends your status or routine: to be unable to find your car keys as you head out the door to an important appointment thrusts you into an experience of liminality, as does receiving the news that a loved one has died, or being involved in a bus accident, or becoming trapped in an elevator. Taking the concept even further, Turner made connections between the "leisure genres of art and entertainment in complex industrial societies and the rituals and myths of archaic, tribal and early agrarian cultures."[40] He argued that these genres were all places where liminal experiences could occur. Unfortunately he didn't write about liminal experiences in worship events. He left that connection for us to make.

We should understand and use this word regularly when talking about designing and curating worship. Content alone doesn't bring transformation. Education isn't the same as, nor does it necessarily lead to, change. Lasting change usually comes from entering into liminal moments that are occupied by God. The theological student at the Stations of the Cross experienced a liminal moment when he encountered the emergency-exit sign.

Recently, I curated three worship events for a group of new ministers. The themes arose from the stories about Elijah in 1 Kings 19. One of the events focused on the idea of running away. A video loop from the movie *Run Lola Run* provided the backdrop as we read about Elijah's depression, fear, faith, and response. I focused on the question God asked Elijah repeatedly whenever he stopped running, "So, tell me, what are you doing here?" I think these were liminal moments for Elijah, and they also provided that kind of space for those worshiping. In worship, liminal moments are more likely to arise from questions than they are from statements.

Some would say that liminality is the condition for hearing and receiving the gospel.[41] This makes it easier to grasp that it isn't possible to create liminal experiences, only to provide situations and settings in which they may occur. Anything more is manipulation.

Liminal moments are often the product of worship elements that allow depth and open-endedness. They don't have to be individualistic. A corporate song or responsive reading, a well-known benediction, or even listening to a sermon can provide corporate moments of liminality for a group in the same way that being stuck in an elevator might. If the worship is moving too fast, those moments of insecurity and uncertainty into which God might speak will be lost.

There is also a level of anxiety attached to any liminal experience. The future is uncertain, outcomes unknown.[42] But liminal experiences are transitory. They can be nothing more. If the lack of norms and the feelings of suspended status last more than a few moments or hours or days (depending on the circumstance), then apprehension and unease set in, and the transition to closure in a new state is disrupted, perhaps for good. Endless liminality is very disturbing and probably psychologically and emotionally destructive.[43] "Intrinsic to enjoying liminality is an expectation of closure, and the sooner the better."[44] Being stuck with others in an elevator that has broken down can be a liminal experience that results in community building, as can becoming lost while hiking with others. Both happen with the expectation of positive resolution. To know that there is no way out leads to a quite different experience. If the movement into anti-structure doesn't continue on through to structure again, it is not an experience of liminality. The result will be trauma and recrimination. Permanent "in-betweenness" is intolerable; some structure needs to emerge at some point. While this being stuck is unlikely to happen in a worship event, it is worthwhile being aware of the power of liminal moments.

COMMUNITAS

The liminal moments of "social anti-structure" that Turner describes lead, when experienced with others, to liberation from social norms and to the positive experience of what he calls *communitas*.[45] The midpoint of transition in a shared ritual, described as the liminal period, is a time when those involved experience a spontaneous shared, unmediated communication. They find a new identity as a group through the shared experience. This communion, triggered and stimulated by the unexpected escape from anticipated routine, transcends class, race, background, employment, education, age, and gender, and is not rational. It is communitas—"an essential and generic human bond."[46] It is what we often talk about as being what a church community should provide.

Temporary escape from routine may create the opportunity to bond with strangers. Such an experience can border on the euphoric and be unforgettable. The Turners wrote, "It is richly charged with affects, mainly pleasurable. It has something magical about it. Those who experience communitas have a feeling of endless power."[47] Victor Turner would later write, "[F]or individuals and groups, social life is a type of dialectical process that involves successive experience of high and low, communitas and structure, homogeneity and differentiation, equality and inequality. . . . In other words, each individual's life experience contains alternating exposure to structure and communitas and to states and transitions."[48] Perhaps this would describe what is most clearly obvious in a Pentecostal worship event.

All forms of communitas move toward being normalized in order to maintain social control. Spontaneity ceases, and order increases. So what was experienced on a pilgrimage or in a service of worship is systematized and organized in order to preserve it. Within this structure, communitas may again arise. Communitas and structure can cycle continuously and can be experienced by individuals or groups. The danger comes when we set out on the endless search for variety or for more powerful encounters with God in our worship, seeking the liminal and the sense of communitas rather than the God who meets us in both.

COMMUNITY

Community is a generic term I use to describe the relationships and feelings of belonging that can come from regular experiences of liminality and communitas. Worship is probably the major builder (or underminer) of community. Communitas builds long-term community. We need to recognize this and become much more aware of how what we do in worship affects the community we are seeking to build. Much of what I have already said could be reiterated here. Participation builds community, introducing leaders in worship by name builds community, ensuring that everyone understands what is happening and what is expected builds community, as does learning a shared benediction or prayer, and so on.

Community demonstrates the Trinitarian nature of God, so what are we demonstrating when we lack community? Strong community is one of the most significant gifts we have to offer those outside of the church. If they feel they could belong, they will come. If they continue to feel they belong, they will stay.

It is pointless and counterproductive to talk about community without offering at least a taste of it. The church and, therefore, churches should be modeling the kingdom of God even if it is in some small and incomplete way. We should ban the use of the word "community" by all worship leaders and curators and have people experience it by building in and on some of the values I have suggested. You can't talk community into being. You can only practice it and model it.

Building the communal memory of a congregation builds their communal identity. Rather than clean out the worship space completely each week, leave some remnants of the previous week— bind written or drawn responses into a book and hang it on the wall for all to read; leave a collective art exploration in place. If you are in a nonliturgical setting, introduce some prayers that are used consistently and can become memorized. Take time each year to remember, reflect on, and talk about the high and low points of the community's life that year. Do it in a worship-event context. (I usually use Christ the King Sunday, the last before Advent, for this.) Use the annual report to have people tell their stories of the past year and how being part of your community of faith has helped or hindered their following of Christ. These strategies not only build communal memory, they help connect those who may have missed the events being referred to.

Probably the deepest longing in Western cultures today is for fulfilling relationships and community, to know and be known, to love and be loved. The church owns that space, but we have neglected it, let our title lapse, sold our birthright. I know it's not easy to build community when most in the congregation don't want it. In fact, it may be impossible (in which case, you should probably leave and start something new). But that's not an excuse to let your worship curating drop to the lowest common denominator. Curate with passion. Curate with heart—a heart for God, a heart for people, and a heart to see those people encounter God in life-transforming ways. Relationships will flow from that. Any other motivation is unworthy of the title "worship curator."

I have a young friend I have known since she was born nine years ago. Her parents were part of the church I was involved in at the time. I left that church four years ago and only see her once a year or so now, but her mom e-mails me about what she is up to as she has life-threatening health problems. Recently I sent my eight-year-old friend a note congratulating her on winning her school speech competition with a speech on mermaids. Her mother heard her say to another adult as she read my card, "See, he still loves me."

That experience affects the way I curate worship. It serves as a reminder that people do care about relationships and that the most unlikely connection can be transforming. It reminds me that small details can be significant catalysts for transformation and that I will usually never know the levels of transformation that are happening for people.

HOSPITALITY

Hospitality is the heart of community. The biblical image for mission is hospitality. Our buildings, worship spaces, people, and patterns of church life need to work together to grow community. They need to be hospitable and promote hospitality. What does it say to people in the church if we lock our buildings most of the week and only allow a few of our congregation to have access keys? Community grows out of hospitality and feeds back into hospitality. Our worship events need to be places of hospitality. This covers the small stuff that is so important. Things like making sure people know what is being asked of them in the worship event, making sure everyone can read, hear, see, and understand what is going on. This is especially true of the stranger among us. Introducing yourself if you are leading something, giving clear instructions, never assuming knowledge or experience with an element of worship or aspect of the Bible or theology. So much of the curation process is about hospitality.

DEPTH AND BREADTH

Spiritual desire is best met when the worship we curate has both *depth* and *breadth*. Too often we settle for shallow and narrow.

In early 2006, I worked with worship curator Cheryl Lawrie and a few others in Melbourne to design and curate worship for Easter

Saturday. Our motivation was to do something interesting for ourselves and that the Saturday was a "dead" day in the midst of Holy Week. We wouldn't be competing with any other church services. We ended up with a very beautiful and engaging service under the title *Dead Man Waiting*. This was the space I mentioned earlier with five stations set around a pile of crushed ice and large blocks of ice. Above it hung a crown of thorns made of red ice that dripped onto the pile below. A large video projection of a man breathing out into the cold air was repeated on two sides of the circular dome roof of the building. The space was lit by the video and black light. The content of the service was five-fold and linked to each of the stations. About forty people turned up. They included the unchurched, dechurched, antichurch, and still churched. The conversation in the bar after indicated that all had found the worship very moving and engaging. God was encountered. Responses were made.

I was very surprised a few weeks later to discover that the Sydney Anglican's magazine and website had picked up on our worship. The reporter used us to illustrate the antibiblical, nonevangelical, style-over substance, shallowness, and evils of the emerging church. As if a church service using 125 kilos of ice would somehow water down the gospel!

Actually the service was far from superficial. It was based on a cycle of repeated reflection on the biblical text John 16:7 and moved through the accepted psychological stages of grief first proposed by Elisabeth Kubler-Ross in 1969: denial, anger, bargaining, depression, and acceptance. I doubt that anyone participating realized the depth of this framework shaping the event. It was beneath it and woven through it, but not overt or referred to.

Breadth comes from having participation by a wide range of people who represent various backgrounds and stages of faith. It involves good explanations and introductions to worship elements, catering to a variety of learning styles, drawing from a range of traditions and subcultures, and new forms and ideas. It sees worship within a broader context of justice, politics, and economics, pointing to worship as life in the real world as local and global followers of Jesus.

Depth and breadth don't come from using greater creativity or better music, from being more relevant or having a better understanding of culture, or even from the arts. The solution to shallowness and narrowness lies in asking better questions. At least that's where the solution starts. We need to start asking better and deeper questions, some of which I have raised in earlier chapters, before we start assuming we know what the answers are. Someone described a religious fundamentalist as a person who gives great answers, but doesn't ask any questions. That is often the way we operate in the church. We don't ask the right questions, and we overlay what we know of the past on what we think we want to do for the future.

In his work with mainly Christian artists for public sacred space installations, worship curator Dave White describes depth as "a close friend but not a lover." His perspective is that *depth* implies complexity and abstraction that can detract from the story, which is the "lover." He wants the biblical story (in the case of the event he is discussing, the Easter story) to be kept simple and uncomplex, and to speak for itself. For Dave, depth comes from the repeated involvement of the same artists year after year, building on their experiences of reflection and collaboration. His perspective is a valuable one, and I don't see it in conflict with what I am saying.

I think depth and breadth are what we are most missing in our search for new forms of worship. I also think they are what most people outside the church would like to find inside it. The open-endedness referred to earlier can contribute to depth. It allows for a layering of possible responses and interpretations that can be accessed by people at the level and context appropriate for them at that time. Depth. You can't always see it. Not everyone will appreciate it, but it adds substance, and some will notice it and be moved by it.

INTERACTIVITY

Brian Eno says he wants his tombstone to read, "Interactive is the wrong word. It should be..." He defines interactive as "unfinished."[49] It's an excellent definition, and one we should take seriously in our curating of worship. The culture has shifted from supplying ready-made, completed artifacts or experiences to ones where we have to— or choose to—finish or complete the experience or artifact as part of our using them. Instead of being limited to just moving through what someone else has produced for us, we want to engage with the material, and there is no longer any right or wrong way to engage. So we mix and match audio and video components, pieces of furniture, clothing, and even belief systems. We no longer expect to only be able to purchase these as completed sets put together by someone else. We want that "finishing" role ourselves. We are becoming (if we haven't already become) both artists/producers and consumers.

Interactivity connects with participation and open-endedness in worship. It says to curators that we need to explore ways within our worship to let participants make choices and decisions, and be involved in "finishing" the worship. Not because choice and consumerism are the goals of worship, but because this is one of the ways that people in the emerging cultures are going to best encounter and engage with God. (Choice and consuming aren't bad in themselves.)

All stations used in worship should be interactive—the worshiper should be completing that station in some way, not just responding to what is already finished. This "completing" might be writing a statement, molding a shape from clay, or hammering a nail into a wooden cross. That particular element of worship is not completed until this work is done by the participant. I would not consider singing songs, listening to a sermon, or spoken responses in liturgy as interactive. These are consumerist activities, completed by someone else for me to consume. It is very easy to encourage passivity when we make changes in our worship. We start using more video clips and recorded music; we create reflective PowerPoint slides or produce a drama. These provide more interesting and creative worship, and they may even be more engaging than previous elements. But they do not necessarily lead to interactivity or active participation.

TERMS THAT SHOULDN'T BE IN THE WORSHIP CURATOR'S VOCABULARY

There are a few words and ideas that get thrown around in church circles that simply need to be excised from the lexicon:

- Relevant: Avoid it at all costs. Don't try to be it. It reeks of a lack of integrity. If you follow the principles I have laid out, it will be the very least of your concerns.

- Different: Never say, "Today we are going to do something a bit different" as a way of introducing an element. That tells people there is a norm, and this isn't it. Instead of inviting response, this phrase invites comparison and critique. Just offer a good segue and clear introduction and move on.

- Don't backpedal: Never say, "I'm sorry, but I haven't had time to organize this properly" or make other preemptive excuses for the events you curate. Either we will know anyway, or we won't notice and you didn't need to say it. These preapologies are meant to lower expectations and prepare people for disappointment. They come out of your own lack of self-awareness and integration. If in your preparation you've asked the right questions and worked hard, get over it and have some integrity and courage. If you haven't, then learn from your mistakes and make it right next time.

There are many other terms that will play into this process of developing a new language for worship. You will add many of your own, terms specific to your personality or situation. An obvious omission from those covered so far is the term *stations*. This concept is so foundational to a new worship vocabulary and language that I give it a chapter of its own (see chapter 8). Before that, there is a final question we need to consider.

7

What Do I Want to Say?

I n chapter 2, I suggested that asking yourself what you understand
to be the purpose of the church and of worship is critical. When
it comes to actually designing a worship event, there is another
critical question: What do you want to say? What do you want the
worship event to say? This means not just in the sermon, or the talk to
the children, but the whole event—from leaving the street to going back
on the street and everything in between. Bruce Ramus, show designer
extraordinaire and lighting director for a number of U2 tours, always
asks himself a particular question when he comes to design a show. He
told me, "[The audience] comes into a concert and out of their worlds.
I take them out of their heads and into their bodies—and hold them
there for the concert. Every song and segue is part of a journey and at
any moment something can happen that cuts across what I want to say
to people on that journey. I always keep my answer to that question in
mind when I work on a show. 'What do I want to say here?' I ask it of
each song and of the whole show. I ask it of those participating in the
show—designers, contributors, and the band."

These words have inspired me to start my worship planning with
that same question. How I answer that question changes with each
worship event. To demonstrate what I mean, I'd like to show you how

I answered it for two different events. The first is for an inherited—or mainstream—church worship service, the second a World Vision staff prayer day at a conference center. Here's how I thought through that question as I planned the worship service:

WHAT DO I WANT TO SAY? (CHURCH WORSHIP EVENT)

- That God loves each person regardless of what he/she has done or how he/she feels about that.
- That Peter's story of denying Jesus three times in John 18 demonstrates how God feels about us.
- That anyone can be a denier at any time. This doesn't have to be the end of a relationship with Jesus.
- That there is no place so dark that God cannot see me; no place so far from him I can't return or that he can't reach me.
- That new starts are always available.
- That a relationship with God through Jesus is more dependent on the character and consistency of God than it is on my character or consistency.
- That a Christian worship event can be accessible to anyone regardless of their stage of spiritual formation.
- That open-ended, reflective, nonlinear, nonsung spaces can provide liminal moments into which God can speak.
- That St. Mary's Church is open to engaging creatively with its community.

Those statements helped me to keep in mind what I wanted to achieve in that church-based event. They also helped me to understand the breadth and significance of my task. I wasn't just "putting a service together."

The difference in physical space, people, and expectations involved in a staff prayer day led to very different answers.

WHAT DO I WANT TO SAY? (PRAYER DAY)

- That Christian worship can be accessible to anyone regardless of a person's stage of spiritual formation.
- That open ended, reflective, non-linear, non-sung spaces can provide liminal moments into which God can speak.
- That World Vision Australia takes its values statement, "we are Christian," seriously.
- That there is much to celebrate in the last year of World Vision Australia's pilgrimage with God among the extreme poor of our world.
- That God celebrates the work we do to alleviate extreme poverty and to help individuals, families, and communities rebuild in sustainable ways.
- That in the same way we celebrate our co-working with God, we can also celebrate the value and importance of our role in this relationship.
- That we therefore can anticipate, expect, and draw on the resources of God to do our work. These resources may be corporate, organizational, or personal.

- That the coming to earth of Jesus is good news/ joy to the nations (Luke 2:10), because in Jesus we have a model of the way God wants to work with the poor/marginalized and therefore the way we need to work as well (Luke 4:18-21).

What do I want to say? An artist asks that question about her art. A filmmaker asks that question about his film; a lighting director asks it of his rock concerts. I think worship curators should ask it of their worship. It isn't always necessary to come up with a clear answer. Often the asking is enough to make you aware of the issues you will need to manage and to work with, and cause you to see what isn't helpful to the task at hand. The question is more important than the answer. How you answer the question helps you evaluate your worship.

GOOD WORSHIP?

It should be coming clear to you by now that I think we should take the preparation and delivery of worship events very seriously. This means they often take up serious time. That commitment can lead curators to wonder if it's worth it. Is there a way to measure the success or effectiveness of worship? Obviously I believe worship can be unsuccessful, so what's the difference between unsuccessful worship and successful worship?

It worries me that we hesitate to evaluate what we do in worship. We somehow assume that because it's worship, God will take anything we offer, and that to evaluate that in any way is somehow just not appropriate. I'm not talking about trying to evaluate or measure the worship of any individual—that can only be known by the individual and God. I'm interested in the degree to which the quality of the curation enables or hinders the worship of individuals and the community. I believe very strongly that the way we curate a public worship event has a huge impact on how people are able to respond to God—to respond to the Trinitarian community of God with heart, soul, mind, and strength. This is true whether you're curating a Sunday morning community service in a cathedral or a citywide art installation in the town square. So it's worth considering the quality and efficacy of what we create. What does "good" worship look, feel, and sound like? What is the desired end result of worship we curate? How do you decide if worship is "good" or "bad"? What do those terms mean in relation to worship? Are they even appropriate?

I try to keep away from using *good* or *bad* to describe worship. I prefer the terms *strong* and *weak*. As a worshiper I evaluate worship as strong if it has a clear shape and flow to it, reflects good theology, engages me with my world, is audible and understandable, and provides me with some space for reflection and response as well as participation. The outcome of these coming together would be that I met with God in some way. Weak worship would be that in which I can't hear clearly, don't know what was expected, is light on biblical story, contains poor theology, is unaware of tradition, and doesn't connect with my world or allow me room to respond or reflect. My assessments aren't related to the genre of the worship, but they are subjective. Many worship leaders I meet work under the assumption that worship has been successful if everyone leaves happy. In his book *Against Happiness*, author Eric Wilson suggests that, "the predominant form of American happiness breeds blandness."[50] That may explain why so much worship is bland. Having a working answer to the question "What is worship?" allows you to move beyond the idea that successful worship leads only to happy people. When you have answered that question with a deeper understanding of what worship can be for your community, you can move away from the idea that people have to respond to God only with joy. You can help your community see that being "up" is not necessarily more Christlike than being "down" and that they don't need to pretend to feel anything other that what they actually feel.

As curator, I determine in advance the success or failure of worship I design. I know whether or not I have put in the time and effort required, if I've taken into account the factors of curating I've described previously and how I delivered on the "What do I want to say?" question. This doesn't mean that the outcome will always be strong worship. If I am curating in an unfamiliar venue or for a community I am not part of, the worship can miss the mark even with all of my careful preparation.

Another factor in determining outcomes is the response of the worshipers—both during and following the event. If I have given the community three stations to use as a response and no one moves to participate in those stations, it may indicate I have misread the community, my instructions weren't clear enough, the responses aren't related closely enough to the content, or some factor beyond my control. It may also be that everyone is responding silently where they are seated, but that would be extremely unusual. (In a community that is not used to moving during worship I would usually model what I wanted by doing it myself early on.)

I don't put much stock in the comments of people as they leave a service. Unless they have sought me out to speak to me, these words are often platitudes and social niceties. I put much more stock in written or spoken comments that come in the days (sometime years!) following a worship event. I often encourage people to respond by e-mail and let me know what was useful to them and what wasn't. As discussed before, worship is ultimately about transformation which may go beyond the worship event, so evaluating it in terms other than those relating to transformation only leads me to deceive myself.

What Do I Want to Say?

I know I can't determine the success of a worship event by counting the accolades of people as they leave (although an ego rub doesn't go unappreciated), and genuine responses, especially those that describe a specific encounter or experience, are a welcome part of any evaluation. But they aren't an accurate evaluation on their own. Also, a minimal response doesn't necessarily indicate poor worship or tell me I could have done better.

The problem with my defining successful or strong worship in terms of the quality of my preparation is that it doesn't hold up as well for worship curated by other people. You may have noticed that I can be quite critical of worship events I attend or participate in. It would be arrogant and presumptuous of me to assume that the curators of those events I have criticized hadn't given it their best. They probably have. Often what they lacked was experience or alternative models or an understanding of some basic principles. So I am in some trouble with my definition.

So let me nuance it a bit. Giving it my best involves measuring myself against a number of elements:

- Understanding the community for which I am curating and the values it holds;
- Staying true to my working definition of worship;
- Analyzing the category of worship required (more on this in chapters 9 and 10);
- Carefully answering the question, "What do I want to say?"
- Collaborating with people I trust to offer me criticism and affirmation;
- Being still long enough and often enough to hear what God is saying to me about what I am doing as I do it;

- Constantly imagining the congregation
  responding—will people know what is expected
  of them at any given point? This helps me
  remember the range of ages and stages present
  and to clarify my instructions and the content;
- Praying and imagining my way through the
  whole event on paper. This helps me see where
  segues and transitions are needed, as well as see
  how the elements flow—or fail to flow;
- Doing the work of exegesis and understanding
  for any biblical text involved.

This process helps me figure out in advance if a particular piece of worship is strong. I am totally dependent on the Holy Spirit turning up and engaging with each person who takes part in the event. I can't engage people with God, but I can set them on a path toward that possibility. To do that I use all the gifts, experience, intuition, creativity, and knowledge that God has given me. In the end, I can do no more except pray that God will step into the gaps and infuse the content on the day.

A few years ago, I was putting together a worship event in the midst of a difficult week. I had watched the lengthy marriages of two sets of friends disintegrate, and another friend was forced out of pastoral leadership in the church he had led for just a couple of years. I was weary. I had too much work with too many deadlines and too many balls in the air over too long a period. In my weariness, a question ran through my mind: What does church have for someone in my situation? A half an hour of singing meant to push me out of my sadness and into something "better"? A sermon giving me another three ways to better follow Jesus that I can add to the hundreds I have collected over the last few years? A stream of people asking me how I am, but not waiting long enough for me to tell them?

I didn't feel like going to church but went anyway. In the midst of my difficult week, I participated in what I would call strong worship. It was good for me in my situation. The preaching wasn't too long (the combined length of two sets of announcements took longer), and it provided a thoughtful perspective of the biblical texts. But the best part was the response time that followed. There were four simple activity stations to wander around as a way of engaging with God. Regardless of where anyone was on the emotional health spectrum that night, they were invited to encounter God with no expectations of any particular response and no comparisons of various responses. There was enough mental headroom in the stations to allow me to engage in ways not necessarily directly connected to the sermon topic.

In that open-ended, ambient environment, I met with God. I think the person sitting next to me, who was very "happy-clappy," also did. We did so, and we were given the opportunity to do so, without any expectation that our responses would in any way correlate to one another's. I didn't come away feeling any better than when I arrived, but I was aware of having glimpsed God's grace and love for me just as I was, in my current state. I felt sustained.

Authentic worship. Empathetic worship curating. An invisible curator. That's good, strong worship, I reckon.

Chapter 8

Stations: The New Altar Call?

harles Finney, an American revival preacher in the 1800s, is credited with starting altar calls. It was, and continues to be, a controversial topic. Those of a Reformed theological position felt that to ask people to come forward was to put undue psychological pressure on them to make a decision that they and God might not be ready for. It was the Spirit's work to bring to "birth" and anything that caused this to happen prematurely was in danger of leading to what they would call "temporary faith" or "a false profession."

Finney was aware of the emotional turmoil people of his day went through before committing to following Christ. He and others made use of the "anxious seat" that led to altar calls as a way of demonstrating the desire of individuals to respond to what God was saying to them. There is nothing intrinsically sacred about an altar call, and there are many other ways to encourage people to respond to what God might be saying to them than to walk to the front or the back of the church for prayer. I want to suggest that an appropriate way to have people in your community respond to God today is the use of stations.

According to the New Catholic Encyclopedia[51] the term *station* had several different usages in the early church, although none has clear origins. The term comes from the Latin *statio*, "to stare" or "to stand." In other words, it means to stand, to stop, to take up a position. Over time, a station came to be understood as gathering at a specific place for a specific purpose. In chapter 11, I'll give a more in-depth history of the Stations of the Cross and how it calls on people to do just that, but for now, it's enough to understand a station as a stopping or standing place, or a place for a particular activity. In worship, a station is simply a designated place in the gathering space where a prescribed activity can happen during a worship event. It could be marked by a small table, a collection of objects, or an image on a wall, floor, or ceiling. Written or spoken instructions let people know what to do when they come to this particular spot in the worship space. Station activity means that most people will be moving around the room and not sitting in their seats. *The purpose of stations is to provide a worshiping community with a variety of options for interacting with the biblical story or theme being presented in the worship event.*

"For those who want to save their life will lose it, and those who lose their life for my sake, and for the sake of the gospel, will save it." Matthew 16:25

Choose a stone from the pile and hold it in your hand for some time. Think about the hard places in your soul. Identify the unnecessary burdens which weigh you down on the journey. When you are ready release your stone into the depths of the water.

Perhaps you've heard of or used prayer stations. These are an example of the stations genre, but I encourage curators to use stations in a much broader way—one in which prayer stations might be a subset. Stations might involve prayer, reflection, meditation; they might also involve heavy lifting, hammering, sawing, yelling, painting, eating, smashing, or setting fire to something. It's important not to emasculate the content of stations or to overfeminize the style of responses. Men often feel that this sort of worship is not for them.

THE PURPOSE OF STATIONS

Using stations in worship means individuals determine the pace and content of their experience depending on their needs and response to the issues raised. This means the worship tends to become interactive and participatory rather than passive and, therefore, has a greater chance of connecting with a greater number of people and providing liminal moments of encounter with God. Stations also allow for people to interact with a theme on a number of levels, and they often generate a more creative and holistic engagement than traditional didactic or linear structures, because of the variety of ritual acts and stimuli involved. People might be invited to write, draw, touch, imagine, reflect, smell, listen, and move at any given station, and this kinesthetic dimension enables participation in the theme in deep and significant ways. This range, likewise, caters to a spread of learning styles, ages, theological experience, and stages of spiritual formation in ways that a sermon alone can't do. In other words, the use of stations provides a vehicle by which the Spirit of God may speak in different ways to different people.

> Tear from the newspaper page the first heading or image that captures your attention. Make this the subject of your prayer. When you are ready, peg your clipping on the clothesline at the front.

The basic format for using stations is to present a theme (biblical or not) in some way, and then provide some designated points of activity in and around the worship space. Each of these offers stimuli and directions for a meditation or activity based on the theme. After a brief introduction to the theme and the layout, participants are free to visit these places on their own, generally in any order and for as long as they wish within a given time frame. They are then free to interact with each station according to the directions and materials provided.

Stations may be used within a regular order of service, or they may be the main focus of the worship event. Almost always, though, stations will need to be framed in some way. For example, within a regular order of service, stations may follow the sermon. In a special event such as a Good Friday or Christmas Eve service, stations may occupy most of the event time but they will still need some sort of introduction and, probably (but not necessarily), a conclusion.

> Song 1:10, 14. "The flowers are springing up and the time of the singing of birds has come. . . . My beloved is a banquet of flowers in the gardens of Engedi."
>
> Choose a flower that reminds you of a time when you have experienced giving or receiving beauty, color, new fruit, or harvest. Appreciate the joy this brought. Thank God flowers are part of the seasons and will come again.
>
> For the children: Choose a flower you like. As you hold it, think about how beautiful or colorful it is. Thank God that you are even more beautiful to God than the flower is.[52]

When setting up stations for a worship event, several important practical details need to be considered.

- The number of different stations can vary, depending on the time available and the breadth of response being sought. More than ten different stations at one time would be unusual. Four to six stations are usually sufficient.

- Stations may be repeated in larger venues for larger groups. The overall number of stations should be determined by the expected size of the congregation. Too few stations for the number of people lead to lines, congestion, and distraction, which lead people to opt out of participating. Too many, and people are overwhelmed by choice and tend to rush from one to the next. The stations need to be spaced far enough apart, so there is room for several people to get near whatever objects or stimuli have been provided.

- Stations can be reused from previous events. Don't assume that you have to do different stations every time you use them. For several years, I used the same stations weekly as a response time following the sermon—communion elements, candles for prayer, and an offering basket.

- Stations can use the same materials or action but be given different content. Lighting a candle, for example, can be used for a multitude of responses. Candle-prayer lighting can be done in several ways: using votives or heating candles, floating candles on water, placing candles in sand trays or in paper bags that are written or drawn on. (Put sand in the base of the bag if you do this.)

- Stations can be linear, cyclic, or nonlinear (ambient).

- *Linear stations* require participants to go through them in a particular order and, generally, to complete the full sequence. Stations of the Cross is an obvious example of linear stations: the story requires a chronological sequence, starting at station one.

- *Cyclic stations* are also linear but can be entered at any point.

- *Nonlinear stations* can be approached in any order or selected at random. Sometimes I describe these as *ambient stations*.

- Worshipers need to be invited to participate and told clearly what to do, not just left hanging around. They need to know roughly how long they have to cover the stations, and that they can choose to do all, or one, or none.

- The directions for the stations either need to be either printed on a single sheet that people carry with them or available in multiple copies at each station.

- Consider providing one or two stations that are not located in a specific place but can be done seated wherever people find themselves. This allows those who find getting up to participate daunting, physically challenging, or unappealing to engage with the theme from their seats and, most importantly, look as if they are participating even if they aren't. (Although I have tended to use the language of instruction and direction when talking about the content of a station, people should always be invited rather than instructed to participate.[53] The difference may appear minor, but it isn't. Providing this level of safety is the role of the curator.)

- Care and thought need to be given to the relevance of any given ritual or action to the theme and to the congregation. Is what people are being invited to do actually going to enable a deeper engagement with the ideas or story? Or is it just an action for the sake of it? Sometimes, connections between the action and the theme need to be made explicit. For example, if the station has a bowl with water and the theme is repentance, it is better to include in the directions a statement such as, "Consider one incident from the last week that you regret. As you wash your hands, imagine that moment being cleansed from you" rather than simply "You might like to wash your hands."

- Effective stations involve an action that leads to emotional engagement. Rather than asking for mental reflection or prayer, the instructions could invite participants to write or draw their prayer of confession on a piece of paper, then burn it or run it through the paper shredder. Or they could write their prayer with lipstick (for its connotations of betrayal) on the communion tablecloth.

- Mood is an important consideration in planning stations. Should the mood be quiet, somber, reflective? Or should the mood be more lighthearted, encouraging people to interact with each other in a more chatty and convivial way as they move through the stations? Decide this in advance, because the mood can be determined to a large extent by the effective use of lighting and sound. Music tracks playing in the background are generally more effective than silence while the stations are visited.

- Priming a few people to make an early move helps to get going with a group not used to moving around in worship.

- Endings are important, too. Depending on the nature of the worship event, bringing everyone back together for a communal action such as a responsive reading, song, or communion would be an appropriate conclusion. Or perhaps the event calls for people to interact with the stations in their own time and leave when they are finished. Either way, this needs to be made clear before the stations start. Most often I use recorded music to signal the end of the response time. Ideally this gives people a few minutes to finish what they are doing before the service continues.

You have about 15 minutes to move around and engage with the stations. When the music changes and directions appear on the screen we will come back together.

Using a single station in worship is also a possibility. Churches that have people come forward for communion are already doing this. While people are moving, why not introduce a second station for them to interact with? The example in a previous chapter of people holding a piece of colored card while they prayed could be considered a single station that doesn't require people to move from their pews. Projecting a piece of art on the main screen and asking people to engage with it from where they are or handing newspapers along the rows to have articles torn out for prayers are other examples of single stations. There are many approaches to using stations in worship.

IMMERSIVE WORSHIP

Interactive stations are more than an accessory to worship. They can be used to create what I call *immersive worship*. New Media guru Lev Manovich believes our culture has moved from what he calls *objective space* to *navigable space*.[54] For instance, where the norm for churchgoers used to be to walk into a space and focus on the band playing at the front, now we might walk into a space that surrounds us with multisensory activity. Even the music, now provided by a concert-styled sound system or a DJ, surrounds us.

This is particularly true of emerging and alternative worship events. While alternative and emerging worship groups have tended to curate worship with no "front" to the space as a reaction against pulpit-led worship, the real desire was to create a more immersive experience for worshipers with room to move within that space. While this desire for worship that engages the whole person may not always be clearly articulated or understood, I believe it lies behind much contemporary thinking about worship.

Manovich calls spaces where a built environment (for example, a church auditorium) is overlaid or augmented by other media (for example, a data projector screen) *augmented spaces* or *augmented reality*. This differentiates it from "virtual reality" that takes place in a space that is not connected to the space the user is in at the time. While Manovich is mostly interested in dynamic digital data as the source of augmentation, I believe his work has useful implications for worship in the kinds of curated spaces we are thinking about. In these new spaces, geometry has become less important. It is no longer necessary to be able to see the preacher at the pulpit in order to engage with the content. The content, while not quite ubiquitous, can be found at many stations in the worship space. Information can be accessed in multiple dimensions. It surrounds the worshiper.

At many points in time and space, the worshiper can engage through audio or video media and assemblage art that is overlaid on the physical space of the church auditorium or of the person. This interaction makes for a more powerful experience than one that is not augmented. It creates an immersive experience.

The installation movement in the art world began in the 1950s and marked a slow transition from two-dimensional art hung on walls to art occupying three-dimensional spaces. Installation art only became a major movement within fine art in the 1990s and continues to be controversial. The similarly timed movement within worship from front, clergy-led to participatory and interactive stations-based worship has been equally controversial. For some, it simply doesn't seem like church.

Creating immersive spaces using stations or installations is often a matter of scale—instead of locating a few stations in part of the space, the stations occupy the whole space in which people move, or they move in and out and around various stations within a larger space. An art-installation-based worship space with multiple stations can move toward being an immersive experience.

Installations, like collections of stations, generally involve strategies such as immersion, exploration, and narrative. When I visited the Holocaust Memorial Museum in Washington, D.C., I was surprised by how rough and rude the security staff were as they scanned my bags and searched me on the way in. When I was inside, the lack of directional signage led to confusion and my getting lost frequently. I sat down to chat with an elderly Jewish man who was a volunteer guide. He explained to me that my reactions to the two situations were exactly what the museum hoped for. The designers of the building and the experience wanted people to feel something of the disorientation and confusion felt by Jews in the Holocaust. This was an immersive narrative experience meant to engage visitors in a deeper way.

For a Good Friday service titled *Dead Man Denied* and based on the story of Peter denying he knew Jesus, my fellow curators and I covered the large, empty front platform in our meeting space with grass turf. We placed a wood-fired grill in the middle of it. The auditorium was blacked out, and ten different stations were set around the edges of the grass. People walked and sat on the grass as they moved between stations. This mildly immersive and multisensory experience helped people explore a biblical story that was also set around a kind of campfire.

BALANCING CONTENT AND CONTEXT

Recently I experienced worship in a beautiful space. The curator had gone to a massive amount of effort to curate a space that was almost overwhelmingly stunning in its detail. The building was nothing special—a 1960s, 120-degree wedge shape built out of concrete blocks. The curator hung huge sheets of handmade paper from wires across the high ceiling. These served as both painting canvases and projection screens. Stacks of shredded paper, a table made from ice, a large flaming centerpiece of pumice stone, twelve potted flax bushes, various soft, colored lighting washes, and several video projectors all contributed to the mystery and wonder of this multilayered environment in which worship was taking place. Several weeks of work had gone into making the works of art and setting up the space. It was a magnificent and fitting recognition of the creativity and beauty of the God we serve.

The worship itself was ambient, open ended, and stations based. After a brief introduction to some of the art and symbolism, people were encouraged to respond in whatever ways they wanted, to whatever they sensed God was saying to them. Not everyone present was Christian. Afterward, an older man who was beyond the fringes of the Christian faith was heard to comment, "I don't know what that was about, but it was bloody good." Other less colorful but no less sincere comments indicated that many people had encountered God in the worship event. A worship curator can't ask for more than that. I love this kind of immersiveinstallation-based worship. Love it. And this was well done.

The weakness of it, for me, was a shallowness of content. I have been known to say that context is more important than content when it comes to worship. I say that mostly for effect, wanting to emphasize the much-neglected context. The strong point of the worship I described above was its context. The weak point was its content. The curator would acknowledge that. He's a conceptual artist and one of the most creative people I know. That's his strength.

I just wasn't quite sure what to grasp onto for reflection during the event. A variety of themes were swirling around, and no particular theme was being addressed. I needed some strong, biblical text to form the backbone of the worship installation and, therefore, give me a reflecting point. In my experience of curating installation worship spaces, many people encounter God in ways I didn't imagine when I put the worship together and on themes not directly connected with the one I put up. That's fine with me. It's how it should be if the Trinitarian community of God is present. But as someone coming in from the outside, I like something to grab onto and work over in my mind and heart—a biblical story, theme, or text to explore, at least as a starting place. This gives what is otherwise unguided and nonlinear worship some shape and content, something to hang my heart on. It's particularly important when non-Christians or newer Christians are engaging in the worship. The content, the story, is what makes our worship Christian. It's what takes it beyond being an art gallery.

Searching for the balance between context and content reminds us that stations also need to be true to the biblical content with which they are connected. Below is an e-mail conversation I had with a friend:

> *E-mail 1:* Hey Mark, this week I am talking about forgiveness. One idea I had for a response station was a kind of confession where they could write down their unforgiveness stuff in sand and rub it out at the end. I was just wondering if you have any other kind of stuff I could do.

> *My Reply:* What sort of station you do depends a bit on what angle of forgiveness you are speaking about. Give me some more clues. If possible, I like to connect my stations with the biblical passage, for example, if I was preaching on Jesus' encounter with the woman caught in adultery, I would use sand as you suggested. The two don't have to be linked, but it gives some integrity and deepens the response if they do. So let me know what passage you are using. Some starters would be: felt pen on small mirrors wiped off with spray; papers written on and burned in a bowl; burning incense; etching sins into a small white or

red candle (that is, scratching with a pin or wire) that is then lit and melts away; writing on rice paper with children's marker pens and dropping the paper into a bowl of water—sometimes it takes a long time to dissolve though! Magic "disappearing paper" works faster but is still slow; scratching on melting blocks of ice. . . . There are lots of possibilities. Let me know the text.

E-mail 2: I was thinking of the passage in Matthew 6:14-15, just after the Lord's Prayer.

My Reply: The Message translation of that says, "In prayer there is a connection between what God does and what you do. You can't get forgiveness from God, for instance, without also forgiving others. If you refuse to do your part, you cut yourself off from God's part." This passage seems to me to be about reciprocity. I think I'd do a two-part station. Part 1: Have each person look in a small mirror tile at themselves and ask, *What do I need God to forgive me for?* Write a word or draw a symbol on the mirror in soap that says what you think God wants from you. Read the Scripture (1 John 1:9). Know that God forgives you. Wipe the soap off and leave the mirror clean.

Part 2 is about "Now that God has forgiven you, is there someone you need to forgive?" Pick up a black stone. Hold it firmly in your hand as you ask God to show you anyone who needs your forgiveness. When you think of someone, release the stone into a bowl of water and pray for God to bless them.

Something like that would work I think.

E-mail 3: Hi Mark, Thanks. The young adults have been saying that using stations takes the service to a deeper level. I'm recruiting a team to help with creative ideas.

Stations don't always have to be connected with biblical texts, and sometimes this can't easily be done, for example, when designing stations on a theme such as winter or spring. But personally I prefer stations that arise from a biblical text.

While stations can be a wonderful tool for worship, they are not to be treated as an easy way to cut down on your service preparation. Using stations well takes considerable care and, therefore, time. They can be a very powerful element in worship and careful pastoral follow-up may be required. They also lend themselves to a wide variety of worship contexts, some of which we'll explore in the next chapter.

9

Contexts for Worship

I find it helpful to think about worship events falling into three clear—albeit somewhat artificial—categories: community worship, transitional worship, and guerrilla worship. I say artificial because these are descriptive labels rather than prescriptive ones. They are arbitrary, but I find them a useful tool for thinking about what may be required when I am curating worship.

Worship that takes place in a church building is what I call *community worship*, as in "the community of faith at worship." This could take place in a warehouse or a function room, but is set in a space that is that community's primary place of regular worship. Its primary aim is to sustain people in their following of Christ in the world by providing them with opportunities to respond to God with heart, soul, mind, and strength. There might be a strong evangelism or mission component to what takes place, but most of those who gather to worship are already followers of Jesus.

Guerrilla worship is found at the other end of the spectrum of familiarity. Aimed primarily at those outside the community of faith, guerrilla worship is almost always located outside of a regular place of community worship. It might be at a festival, a gallery opening, or in a public square. It has an element of the subversive to it.

Somewhere between the two is what I call *transitional worship*. This could be youth-group worship where a significant number of the participants are unchurched, or a gathering of street people, or the community of faith meeting in a third space. It basically scoops up everything that doesn't quite fit in the community or guerrilla worship categories. I'll explain and illustrate each category in this and the next chapter.

Regardless of the category, you need a process to work through as you curate. The same process can apply regardless of the context and the order of service. What will change is how each element is aggregated and curated according to the context.

Without a process, there's a tendency to repeat what is familiar by way of pattern and style, to transfer it to another context and assume it will be strong worship in that new context. For example, most outdoor worship I've experienced has involved a church community taking its regular service and doing it outside. All that's missing are the pews. The assumption is that nonchurched people will participate and be attracted simply because we are worshiping outdoors, that changing the context will change the outcome. If the intention is simply to give the existing community some sunshine, or to have them feel what it might be like for an outsider coming into their worship, the result could be a strong worship event. But if the intention is to draw in new people, or draw the Christian community into a deeper relationship with God, or to engage with some aspect of the contemporary culture, it will likely be a disappointment. Context is very important.

Thinking about the context for worship involves far more than just location. It's a process of discernment that pulls together all the concepts I've talked about so far. That process might look like this, starting with the prior questions:

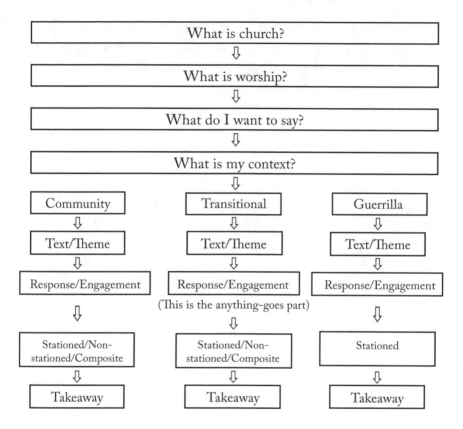

Regardless of the context, style, or setting for the event, this process will make it easier to come up with a worship event that is appropriate and creative. While the week-by-week community worship may not require working through the process every week, transitional and guerrilla events will.

THE CONTEXT OF COMMUNITY WORSHIP

I have little time for the label *contemporary worship*. I find it meaningless. All worship should be contextualized to the community participating in the event. That in itself makes it contemporary in that it happens at the same time and occurs in the present, using both definitions of the word *contemporary*. Where this contextualizing is occurring, I have no intention of trying to change the style of anyone's worship event. If the worship style you have enables the people who gather to engage with God, if it sustains them in their following of Christ in the world, there is nothing to change. It might not be a style that suits me, but that is of no consequence. There will probably always be ways to strengthen it further, and I hope your community engages in regular evaluations that ask hard questions about who you are as a community and how your worship reflects and challenges that sense of identity and the values you hold.

My experience as a pastoral leader has been primarily in Baptist churches. We don't do liturgy; we don't have a fixed order of service; we don't do ritual—except we do all of those things. There might not be much consistency across our denomination, but every Baptist church has its fixed liturgy, order of service, and rituals. The easiest way to find out what they are is to suggest making some changes to the way the service was run last week: preach before the singing, have less singing, announce the offering as a response to the sermon, ask people to get up and move to take communion. See what the reaction is. We have rituals and liturgy, whether we call them that or not.

The aim of community worship is to build a stronger worshiping community so that individuals and groups can better engage with issues outside of the church and work with God to build the kingdom of God. Worship should never be an end in itself.

Neither should any worship event require a commitment to the institution of the church. Our commitment is to following Christ, to serving Christ and the world, and to building relationships. The church exists to sustain us, not suck us dry. I'm not a great believer in expecting everyone to be part of a small group, or attend meetings beyond worship services or even to attending those regularly. I believe most people attend the church they do mainly out of habit or because of the relationships they have there. Those two factors will trump weak worship, poor leadership, and abuse of authority for a very long time before someone moves on.

As a pastoral leader, I'm a minimalist about what should be part of church life and, therefore, what is part of the worship life of a community. I am happy encouraging people to not attend if they are already overwhelmed with work or study pressures, or to take a sabbatical if they are struggling with their faith and finding worship events unhelpful. I also encourage them to let me know when this is happening, so I can suggest readings and appropriate spiritual disciplines, pray for them, and keep in touch with them from time to time. It should be possible to be considered and to consider yourself part of a particular community of faith, even from an emotional or geographic distance. We do that for people moving toward faith, why not for those moving away?

THE PRACTICES OF COMMUNITY WORSHIP

I say all of this because it serves as a background for what I want to say about curating a community-worship event.

In early 2005, I was involved in the start-up of a new worshiping community in downtown Melbourne. We created a list of values that seemed important as we began this venture. What started as a short list quickly grew to be quite involved. The list is included here in full to give you an idea of the issues that should be considered when designing a worship event in the context of the values of the church community.

At Urban Seed:church we will:

1. Make a deliberate and sustained effort to resource Christian spirituality among people who consider themselves to be postmodern or part of the emerging cultural milieu.

2. Exist only to sustain our community in following Christ in the world and actively decline to institutionalize that.

3. Cease to exist if at any point the gathered community no longer finds Urban Seed:church helpful or sustaining of them. Programs and projects that lack leadership or support will cease immediately no matter how important they are seen to be by others.

4. Shape everything we do according to the goal of "sustaining and resourcing Christian spirituality in the world."

5. Offer a smorgasbord of resourcing events for our community but have low expectations of anyone as to attendance and participation at any event.

6. Create a fluid and liquid form of church and church life that is creative about how it resources Christian spirituality for groups and individuals within and outside our gathered community.

7. See our community in the broadest terms— that is those connected by geography, interest, Internet, occasional attendance, attendance at specific resourcing events.

8. Be committed more strongly to encouraging spiritual desire than meeting spiritual needs.

9. Encourage spiritual consumerism and a smorgasbord approach to nurturing Christian formation.

10. Understand that the Sunday worship event is only one element among many resources offered to worshipers and to the wider community.

11. Assume in everything we do and say that someone listening/reading/observing/participating doesn't have the background to understand or participate fully without clear explanation and nonjargoned gender-sensitive language.

12. Have a raw urban edge and feel to what we do. We will be risk takers and boundary pushers in worship, mission, and ministry. We will be involved in the marketplace of work, leisure, and the arts in the Melbourne Central Business District.

13. Strongly value and encourage the integration of creativity and the arts in all aspects of our life and worship.

14. Be trusting and strongly committed to artists in all fields of creative endeavor, looking for uncensored and noncontrolling ways to have them use their gifts to communicate and interpret the message of the gospel as they see it.

15. Be irrevocably committed to a model of worship curators, who will enable multiple people to participate in leading elements of the set pattern

of worship each week, and constantly invite and encourage participation in leadership by any member of the community in any aspect of worship.

16. Encourage participation that is given authority as well as responsibility and that can literally shape the community. This includes preaching, which will be contained in the middle of the service of worship and not given elevation in significance above any other element of worship.

17. Expect that the stuff of the everyday lives and cultures of members of the community will be incorporated into our worship through music, movies, passions, hobbies, pastimes, stories, and objects. Worship might not include singing and is more likely to include a recorded track by Tom Waits than Hillsong.

18. Shape its overall pattern of worship around the Christian calender.

19. Draw on the best of historical and traditional practices of Christianity, reframing them for contemporary practice.

20. Encourage anyone in the community to start any project, small group, mission, or ministry at any time without any hurdle or process beyond announcing that intention to the community.

21. Own and fund no programs or projects beyond its worship and administrative life. Funding beyond this will be the responsibility of individuals and

groups within the community who have the vision and call to do something.

22. Appreciate beauty.

23. Be institutionally minimalist and actively committed to minimizing institutional inertia and, therefore, create structures only when they are deemed by the community to be needed, and in a form that best meets those needs at the time rather than follows traditional institutional expectations.

24. See no distinction between clergy and laity in authority or practice.

25. Be committed to grace and listening.

26. Be hospitable and welcoming to the stranger and to the known.

27. Not mind controversy or difference in dress, theology, or perspective, and encourage a variety of opinion and expression in worship and all aspects of the life of the community.

28. Provide a safe place for struggle, failure, and to be one's self.

29. Be committed to exploring questions rather than giving answers: "Thinking allowed. Thinking aloud allowed."

30. Integrate awareness of and response to issues of justice, ecology, and politics into our worship and teaching/preaching.

31. Have a high view of the Eucharist.

32. Celebrate the Eucharist weekly.

33. Be Christocentric. Theologically conservative at our core.

34. Provide pastoral care and a range of ritual-making services to our congregation and broader community.

35. Put minimal pressure on any of our members to do or be anything or attend anything.

36. Take seriously the demise of Christendom, and the postmodern, secularized multifaith environment in which we, and our people, live, move, and have our being.

37. Seek to party extremely well.

This list was, in effect, our answer to the questions discussed earlier. It was an attempt to communicate the ethos of what we were starting to people who had no other models than the very traditional inherited churches they had been part of. It was a difficult process. Whenever just a few values and practices were mentioned people inevitably said, "Oh yes, our church values that too." Many churches could agree to a number of the values listed. For a variety of reasons, very few would be willing to agree to all of them—and there's nothing wrong with that. These were the values that *we* held important and wanted to retain in any worshiping community we were part of. They were the starting point as we curated worship in this setting. It was our answering of the question: "What do we want to say?" So once the values were established, it was time to design the worship.

Elements of a Community Worship Event

Most community worship is linear in nature—the elements follow one another in order—and there is tremendous benefit to having a predictable, regular set of elements. The variety and creativity comes not from a constant changing of the order but from how the elements are executed.

To move toward strong worship, I think the following minimal elements need to be regularly included, though not necessarily in this order:

- Prelude
- Gathering/Call to Worship/Convocation
- Songs/Meditations
- Invocation/Acknowledging the Presence of God
- Prayer of Confession/Declaration of Forgiveness/Words of Absolution
- Scripture
- Sermon/Homily/Rant
- Response
- Communion/Eucharist/Lord's Supper (Words of Institution/Stories of Grace/Elements)
- Concerns of the Church/Notices/ Announcements
- Prayers for Others/Intercessions
- Offering
- Sending Out/Benediction
- Postlude

Even if you don't use that terminology, the content each term describes has an important contribution to make to strong worship.

If your public corporate worship doesn't include most of these elements in one way or another, you should at least do some research and find out more about what you're leaving out and the ways in which you may be selling your community short.[55] The content and emphasis of each element will vary from church to church, and it is this freedom and creativity that can make two similar orders of service look radically different as worship events. To facilitate the consistent introduction of new people into curating elements of the service, I produced a worship handbook for our community that described the values behind our worship events and gave a rundown of what was expected from each element of the service. For example under call to worship it read:

> The call to worship has the function of raising the question "Why are we here?" and enables the congregation to acknowledge the presence of God among us. It is not calling on God to be present in our worship. It is reminding us that we are about to begin corporate worship of God.
>
> Introduce yourself by name. Then offer a Scripture reading, popular song, recorded music, reflection, video clip, poem, hymn, drama, piece of art, story, or ritual action that draws us together. What you do should be clear and decisive in calling the congregation together to worship God. It should be delivered with strength and clarity of voice so that there is no doubt that our corporate worship is about to begin or about what you want us to do.[56]

The need for clarity of purpose was driven home for me when I visited a church in another town. I arrived seven minutes after the advertised starting time and was directed by a sign to go around the side of the building (no cover from the rain). There, another sign advised me to ring a bell, and I would be let in. Eventually I was. The service "started" (late) with someone talking about the latest computer game they were playing, then a band led us in four songs. This was followed by someone talking about an upcoming missions conference, after which we heard a forty-minute sermon on grace. The service wrapped up with ten minutes of notices about upcoming events. Somewhere in there the offering was taken. I felt out of place and completely lost most of the time. It was a very cold winter's evening and there was no heating in the large room. (They tried, but the gas heaters wouldn't work.) We occupied about 30 of the 150 chairs around tables in the space.

This was a typical service for this community. What scares me is I later learned that the way this service unfolded was deliberate. It was planned to be that way. They have adopted what they call a " magazine approach" to worship. This means they have distinct elements that are meant to be unrelated to each other. But most magazines have at least a theme that runs through them and a table of contents to guide you. This service felt random, scattered, and unwelcoming. I was disengaged from God and found it impossible to offer my worship.

A service doesn't have to be stiff and staid to have a sense of purpose and intentionality. The magazine-style service, above, could work if there was an overarching idea or shape to it, a consistent curator of some sort, or even an introductory explanation of the approach itself to guide participants through the various elements.

Curation that develops a sense of purpose in a worship event begins with an understanding of the function of each element in worship.

Knowing those functions allows the curator to make thoughtful decisions about which elements to include in a given worship event and how to arrange them.

Gathering/Call to Worship/Convocation[57]

In her book *Finding Words for Worship*, Ruth Duck writes, "Instrumental music, visual art, and the architectural space create expectations for worship before any words are spoken. An opening hymn involves a congregation in praising God. The first spoken words also help to set the tone and express the purpose of corporate worship: forming and renewing our relationship with God and one another through acts of praise, prayer, proclamation and commitment."[58] According to Duck, the call to worship has the function of raising the question, "Why are we here?" and enables the congregation to acknowledge the presence of God among them.

Generally, the first formal part of the service is a call to worship. There are many aspects to this call. On the one hand we invite God to be among us, which is not to say that God is not present until we start the service. Rather, we voice some hope or desire that our worship will bring us a more intense awareness of God in our midst, and the hope that God will act to transform and renew us through the shared experience of the service. It's not a place for the prayer I recently heard, "Lord, help us to leave all the cares and pressures of the week at the door, so we can focus solely on you." Worship invites God into the cares and pressures of our lives.

We call ourselves and each other to worship. We acknowledge that the service does not happen in isolation from the rest of our lives. We each arrive at church carrying within us the scramble of events, interactions, and feelings that have been part of the rest of the week.

When we call each other to worship, we do not ask people to leave their real lives behind and focus on God instead. Rather, we take time to notice how we are feeling and what issues we bring into the space. And then, assisted by the action or words chosen by the leader, we place those feelings and issues into the context of our shared faith and hope for them to be stilled, stirred, or transformed through our encounter with God and each other.

In practical terms, the call to worship clearly demarcates the beginning of the worship event, so it needs to be clear and strong. People need to know we've started. The call to worship should also signal the transition of consciousness from work or home life to a different experience of time and space.

Songs/Meditations

This part of the service is meant to deepen worship through singing, ritual actions, or reflection on music, images, or texts. It could take place in one block of time or scattered throughout the worship event. The aim is to create the opportunity for a congregational response to God and to encourage our renewed awareness or sense of God.

It's sometimes hard to find songs or meditations that meet the congregation's needs and expectations because of the vastly different ways people have of engaging with God. What works for some people can be completely alienating to others. Those who are more introverted might value more inward contemplation; more extroverted personalities might prefer group or interactive approaches. There is also the question of whether the worship meets us in our intelligence and our thinking as well as engaging with, and allowing us to express, our emotions. We should be actively aware of the various personalities and stages of spiritual formation represented in the congregation. Don't try to cover all bases in every service but aim to do so over time and through the variety of worship events you offer.

Other than songs, this section can make use of rituals, silence, recorded music, symbols, images, and text. There can be a high level of interaction, such as involving the congregation in writing, drawing, moving, lighting a candle, and so on. It is important to provide content for people to engage with in these activities. Some expressions of alternative worship can have an interesting form and involve a range of multimedia tricks, but offer little in the way of "food" for the participants.

Pacing this section requires that the person curating it is sensitive to the mood and level of engagement of the congregation. It helps if there is a high degree of clarity in any explanation, so the congregation is allowed to notice God and pursue their own reflections without confusion or interruption. There is value in having some repetition from week to week, so that over time people can become familiar with songs or texts, and go deeper into them, rather than learning something new each time.

Prayer of Confession/Declaration of Forgiveness/Words of Absolution

I often find that people are resistant to confession as a regular element in worship because they have misunderstood what it could look like. They associate confession with things Roman Catholic. Confession is not primarily a shopping list of bad thoughts, words, and deeds you or others are supposed to have done, although confession of specifics has its place. Rather, confession is the recognition that there are basic patterns or attitudes that block our spiritual growth, and these need recognizing and dealing with. Some people work within a sin-and-redemption framework as their main understanding of salvation. Others have rejected the way guilt has been used by the church to manipulate their emotions and responses. Some people's sin lies in a legacy of hurting themselves and making their own lives small, rather than hurting others. In that context, promoting realistic self-esteem and affirmation is more important than exploring pride and selfishness that are often considered the source of sin in church confessions. Regardless of how you understand sin, Scripture encourages us to confess in order to be forgiven by a faithful and just God who leaves us in a better condition than we were found. So a prayer of confession is included in the order of service.

It's rare to hear a prayer of confession in a church that doesn't come out of a liturgical tradition. These well-crafted prayers of confession are a rich resource from which curators can and should draw. If you move away from the safety of tried-and-true words such as those of a denominational prayer book, do so with care. Ruth Duck raises some interesting issues[59]—to which I've added some of my own—that need to be considered by someone leading others in a prayer of confession. In planning a time of confession, think about:

- Questions of the general and the specific: Unison prayers need to be quite general if they are to be spoken honestly by those praying because people experience sin in different ways.

- The challenge of liberation theologies not just to pray confessions but to commit to change—calling for justice and healing for the victims of sin.

- Questions of the personal and the corporate. Do we need to confess on behalf of a group we are part of?

- The role of corporate confession not only on behalf of individuals but also whole churches and societies. Duck asks, "How does one write a unison prayer of confession, when oppressor and oppressed intertwine not only in one congregation, but often in one person, who may both suffer injustice and do injustice to others?"[60]

- The use of phrases beginning with "if" and "when" that honor the variety of the congregation members' experiences, as not all statements will be true of all people all of the time.

- The benefit of a period of silent reflection after some generalized starter statements that let people explore their experience within guided parameters.

It is important for prayers of confession to include the announcement of God's forgiveness and acceptance—you don't want to leave people in a place of acknowledgement of wrong but rather lead out from there into hope and resolution. The most usual pattern is a declaration based on 1 John 1:9. I might reframe that to say something like, "We thank you Lord that you have said that when we confess our sins you can be relied on absolutely to forgive us, and to remove their residue from contaminating our lives. We live confident in that assurance."

As with all elements of a worship event, there are many different ways to engage people in prayers of confession—monologue, responsive prayer, ritual action, station, and recorded or sung music.

Communion/Eucharist/Lord's Supper

Those of us in "nonliturgical" churches really need to do some work on our understanding of this ritual and how we can best integrate it into our worship events in ways that have integrity for our communities. It needs to be a much more significant and regular event in many Protestant churches. This is my perspective as a pastoral leader not connected with a liturgical church and not particularly concerned with the jot-and-tittle arguments that swirl around this ritual. I have what many would describe as a low-church view of communion. But in my circles, it's a pretty high view!

In my experience with New Zealand Baptist churches, we seem to have put so much focus on the symbolic meaning of the meal that it has become thin and virtually without meaning. In our desire to make sure nothing Roman Catholic sneaks in around the edges, we have lost any opportunity to encounter the risen Christ in a transforming way. This book is not the place for a discussion of the theology of the Eucharist, but that discussion needs to be had by those of us involved in pastoral leadership in the emerging culture with its desire for mystery, relationship, and transformative faith.[61]

Recently I was asked to curate the communion slot at the independent Pentecostal church I attend from time to time. In my opinion, this community hasn't found an approach to communion that fits who they are—it's over in two or three minutes. No explanation is given, and the people are provided only very basic instructions to move to one of two small tables set up with a chalice and bread and to take bread and wine if they want.

In the hopes of landing on something more meaningful, I set up three stations on the usual tables in their usual places, each with a candle, a cross, small glasses, and a jug of cold water. I lit the candles as the congregation sang a song, then talked about the times we see Jesus eating with sinners and outcasts in the Bible. I transitioned into a short explanation of the Last Supper, then read a few verses from 1 Corinthians 11. This was a few weeks before Easter, and our Lenten studies had focused on the health problems caused by unsafe water in the developing world. It seemed natural to tie that discussion into the use of water in communion. I broke the bread, poured the water, then invited all people to come forward while we listened to a recording of opera singer Kathleen Battle singing, "Were You There When They Crucified My Lord?" It was quite basic, but it allowed me to connect with what people were used to as well as move us a bit toward some new ways of thinking about communion.

Three interesting things happened that day. First, the sound technician came up to me before the service and asked if I had given him the right track to play. There was only one track on the disc I gave him. He couldn't comprehend an unaccompanied opera voice being used in worship. Then the song leader put her cup of coffee on the small table in front of her, the same table on which I had laid out the communion elements, candle, and so on. She had to move my jug and cups to get enough room for it. She apparently had no sense of what communion was about or the idea that this might be sacred space. The third thing was that a number of people spoke to me after about how meaningful the communion segment had been, including the service coordinator who marveled at how much work I had done and all the gear I had brought in for such a short slot in the service. I hadn't done much, but it was more than had been done before. Her comments showed me how little value was being placed on the elements of the worship event, particularly on this one.

Whenever possible, I like to have people get out of their seats to take communion. I also like to place communion after the sermon in the order of worship. This allows time to reflect and respond to the opening of the Scripture and what has gone on so far in the worship event.

As you consider where to place communion in your service, think about the overall flow of the event. Make sure you leave a good block of time, so it doesn't feel rushed or tangential to the rest of the service.

Because people are already moving around the space and are in a reflective mode, it makes sense to combine communion with prayer actions such as candle lighting or writing and hanging prayers. I often set out sand trays, each with a central lit candle, and baskets of votive candles. People can pass by the sand trays and light a candle to symbolize a prayer, either on their way to the communion table, or on their way back to their seats. Part of the effectiveness of this is again linked to the response dimension of communion. As we reflect on what Christ means to us and renew our awareness of the community of Christ's body in the church, a natural and helpful outworking of our reflections is to offer prayer, either for ourselves or others.

The words and actions in the lead up to communion are important. Those who curate this part of the service are encouraged to take their time, to pay attention to the overall mood of the congregation, and to be aware of how their demeanor affects the tone of the ritual.

Introduce communion with a suggestion for a particular "way in" to the ritual. Those of us who have been in the church for a long time have participated in communion so often that it can be helpful to have some specific stimulus or hook to direct our reflections. This might be contemplation of Jesus' death on the cross, the idea of sharing in Jesus' new life, being part of Jesus' body, being a member of a church community, the concept of sacrifice or commitment, and so on. Over time, it's helpful to have a balance between the inward and personal (my relationship to Jesus) and the outward and communal (my relationship to others).

For the words of institution, you can use the familiar text from 1 Corinthians 11 or from one of the gospels and physically break the bread and pour the wine as you speak. Consider where you will include prayer to acknowledge God's gift of the person of Jesus, to thank God for gathering the community together as the body, and to ask God to meet people as they take the bread and wine.

Remind the congregation how communion will take place—even if most of them already know, you will likely have visitors and you want them to know what to do. Based on who was present at the Last Supper and the many meals Jesus shared with notorious "sinners," I practice an open table that does not require people to be baptized or even necessarily Christian believers before they can take communion. Whether you practice an open table or not, choose words that indicate that taking communion is a meaningful act between us and God and, therefore, not to be taken lightly. Then give a clear cue—words, music, or a change of lighting—that lets people know when to start moving.

Communion is a representative act, not a magical one, yet there is enormous power in symbol. There is a real mystery in the way taking communion enables us to encounter Jesus and participate in his death and life. God is present to us in our taking the bread and the wine in a profound and ultimately inexplicable way. How you lead communion and what you say will reflect your understanding of the initial event.

Concerns of the Church/Notices/Announcements

The significance of this element of worship in building community is hugely underrated. If we make this a time when anyone can bring a notice to the attention of the congregation about a party they're having, a household item they're giving away, a meeting that is coming up, it can be a major factor in building community. For that reason, I prefer to use the term *concerns of the church* rather than *notices* as it allows for a wide variety of issues to be raised by different people.

Maybe it's difficult in a large church, but most of our events are small enough to have people call out from where they are sitting. In a larger church, concerns can be written in a book before the service and read out at the appropriate time.

Prayers for Others/Intercessions

When I curate worship, I like to have prayers for others run on from the previous segment, concerns of the church. Although it might be led by a different person, the concerns often overlap.

We engage in prayers for others with the assumption that God is present and active in people's lives. As a church, it is important for us to look outward from our lives as individuals and focus on the places and situations, both far away and in the context of our community, where we see and desire to see God at work in the lives of others.

Prayer for others is about consciously attending to the presence of God in the context of our concerns for a person, place, or event. It's bringing others—through prayer—into our personal circle of relationship with God. The prayer doesn't have to be verbal. Prayers for others can take the form of drawing, visualizing, lighting a candle, writing a name, or planting a seed. Consciously attending is about heightened awareness, a renewed quality of attention to the needs of others, in whatever form that takes. As segment curator, you might verbalize the community's prayers after hearing and listening to them. Or you might have everyone pray in silence, you might read a prayer and ask for a verbal response, or you might suggest some kind of kinesthetic response such as kneeling or other prayer postures.

This is an element that calls for collaboration. People often want to speak to the gathered community about their prayer concern. Just naming the issue has a valuable effect for some people, and sometimes the "answer" to the prayer resides in the offers of assistance that arise from the congregation as a result of hearing a need. For others, hearing someone else frame their concern as a worded prayer to God is important. The scope of prayers for others is not limited to needs in the congregation, but includes national, international, and community issues that are significant to the people present as well as items of joy and gratitude.

Kathleen Norris portrays beautifully the value of this aspect of a church service in her book *The Cloister Walk*:

> At the worship services of Hope and Spencer there's a time after the sermon and before the Lord's Prayer, in which people are asked to speak of any particular joys they might wish to share with the congregation, or concerns they want us to address in our communal prayer on that Sunday and also to pray over during the coming week. It's an invaluable part of our worship, a chance to discover things you didn't know: that the young woman sitting in the pew in front of you is desperately worried about her gravely ill brother in Oregon, that the widower in his eighties sitting across the aisle is overjoyed at the birth of his first great-grandchild.
>
> It's useful news as well; I'm one of many who makes notes on my church bulletin; so and so's in hospital; send a card, plan a visit. Our worship sometimes goes into a kind of suspended animation as people speak in great detail about the medical condition of their friends or relatives. We wince; we squirm; we sigh; and it's good for us. Moments like this are when the congregation is reminded of something that all

pastors know; that listening is often the major part of ministry.

I sometimes feel that these moments are the heart of our worship. What I think of as the vertical dimension of Presbyterian worship—the hymns, the bible readings, the sermon—finds a strong and (necessary) complement in the localized, horizontal dimension of these simple statements of "joys and concerns."[62]

Sending Out/Benediction

In most Protestant churches, the final words in the service have two main functions: first, they encourage people to continue following Jesus in the world throughout the week, and, second, they allow us to bless one another in God's name.

Before the benediction, you might have a sending-out song with lyrics that describe the congregation's hopes and intentions about living as Christians in the world. It might not be liturgically correct, but I like the community to say the benediction to each other rather than waiting in silence while it is pronounced by the pastor or service curator. The benediction is a declaration that God loves us. It's not another prayer; it's not asking God to be good to us. It is our final act of worship together before we go out into the world. It declares that we do not go alone, but we go with God.

In my Baptist tradition, we don't have a lot of common practices, the kind that bind us together week after week. If we use the Lord's Prayer, it could be any one of half a dozen different versions so we never get to know it by heart. I've found that using the same benediction until it's well known adds depth to congregational life. Even if we are mostly reading it, I generally divide the congregation in half along various lines: male/female, crunchy/smooth peanut butter eaters, vegetable/meat preferences, or something equally lighthearted. We speak the benediction alternately from one half to the other. People are encouraged to look at one another to receive the words that are spoken. This gets easier when most know the benediction by heart. For those who don't, it's printed in the newsletter each week.

The benediction that has become known as the "Cityside Benediction" was written by Diane Karay Tripp who has generously given her permission for it to be reproduced and used widely.

Cityside Benediction

You are God's servants,
  gifted with dreams and visions.
Upon you rests the grace of God like flames of fire.
Love and serve the Lord in the strength of the
  Spirit.
May the deep peace of Christ be with you,
  the strong arms of God sustain you,
  and the power of the Holy Spirit strengthen
  you in every way.
Amen[63]

Understanding what has traditionally been included in a worship service and what each element is about means you can include and omit, aggregate and eliminate with greater confidence that the overall structure will be helpful to people as they engage with God, with heart, soul, mind, and strength.

There is much debate about how missional or evangelistic worship should be, and I certainly don't intend to add to that debate here. What I will say is that while the word *emerging* may well describe a current style and place in history, the word *missional* should be part of our DNA as Christians. Our worship should undergird and sustain the community at mission in the world. In the words of David Bosch, "The primary purpose of the *missiones ecclesiae* [mission activities of the church] can therefore not simply be the planting of churches or the saving of souls; rather, it has to be service to the *missio Dei* [mission of God], representing God in and over against the world. . .in a ceaseless celebration of the Feast of the Epiphany."[64]

The purpose of curated community worship is to better enable the community to do just that.

10

Guerrilla and Transitional Worship

While most people will be familiar with what I have called community worship, my other contexts or categories may be less familiar. In fact, you may feel that I have already covered all the contexts for worship there are. I find that creating other categories helps me to clarify what the different worship events are trying to achieve and, therefore, to better curate them. Guerrilla and transitional worship may not look much like community worship, but most of the principles and processes are very similar for all types of worship events. What follows builds on the previous chapter rather than sweeping it aside.

GUERRILLA WORSHIP

At the other end of the continuum from community worship lies guerrilla worship. Again this is an arbitrary category. *Guerrilla* is a relatively new word, having only entered the English language in the nineteenth century to describe a soldier of an irregular armed force that fights against a stronger force by sabotage and harassment. The word is Spanish for "little war," and was used for the local resistance against Napoleon's invasion of Spain.

Perhaps its connection to worship, and why I use it, is better understood by looking at what is known as guerrilla marketing. This term was coined by Jay Conrad Levinson in his 1984 book of the same name. He describes an unconventional way of promoting a product that depends on time and imagination rather than a large budget. The term has come to include the huge variety of nontraditional and unconventional uses of media and marketing such as viral marketing, product placement, buzz marketing, and ambient marketing. These undermine mainstream media and approach the marketplace at a grassroots level. I would like to think that the church can be creative and innovative enough to promote the gospel in the marketplace in ways that subvert both empire and common perceptions of what church is about.

In the introduction to her very useful little book, *The Guerilla Art Kit*,[65] Keri Smith writes, "Guerilla art is for everyone. It engages viewers who might never step foot in a gallery. It is free and accessible."[66] The same could be said of guerrilla worship. I use the term to describe worship that generally takes place not in a church building but in a public space, indoors or outdoors. It takes place in space curated with the expectation that the general public will participate along with followers of Christ. There is no expectation on the part of the curator that anyone will be Christian.

We could easily have a lengthy and unproductive debate about whether or not what happens in these spaces is actually worship. My straightforward response would be that people don't have to realize that they are encountering and engaging with the Triune God in order for worship to take place. This can be difficult to get your head around if your experience of worship is limited to people in church buildings.

I know of a middle-aged man who got out of his car at five o'clock in the morning and walked across the grass to a public art installation in the center of a city park. The installation was called the *Christmas Journey of Peace*,[67] curated by Pete Majendie in New Zealand. It was a straw-bale labyrinth with various stations inside it, each dealing with an aspect of peace—global, national, personal, and spiritual. After forty minutes of solitude and reflection, the man stopped to chat with the person on duty. The man explained that he had been an undercover police officer and that for several months he had been carrying a letter in the glove box of his car. In the letter, addressed to his superiors, the officer admitted to repeated perjury and evidence tampering thirty years earlier. He told the volunteer that the *Christmas Journey* had affected him so deeply, he was ready to send the letter. And he did. A month later the national media reported his confession and arrest. He was not a Christian, but he encountered God in a transformative way. Was it in a worship context? That depends on your definition.

That's why I sometimes refer to guerrilla-worship events as "sacred spaces in public places." I believe worship preparation is primarily about offering *context* rather than *content*. The balance between context and content is important, but no straightforward measure of the two exists. In guerrilla worship, context is perhaps more significant than it is in other categories, the context being an environment in which heart, soul, mind, and strength all have opportunity to respond to God. Guerrilla worship is about providing, designing, and curating those contexts.

In *Liquid Church,* Pete Ward writes:

> Moltmann argues that we need to take the informal experiences of people seriously as an arena where the Spirit of God may be at work. If we contain God within the church or if we suggest that the

Spirit is able to work only through a particular kind of preaching, then we limit God. . . . The continual assertion that God's Spirit is bound to the church, its word and sacraments, its authority, its institutions and ministries impoverishes the congregations. It empties the churches, while the Spirit emigrates to the spontaneous groups and personal experience.[68]

Worship inside the church building must support and sustain a faith that is lived out in the push and shove of justice seeking and spiritual desire on the streets and neighborhoods where we live.

CREATING SACRED SPACES

There is a void in our Western cultures where mystery, ritual, and community should be. These are all key features of Christianity, but somehow the church has abdicated that space in our culture. It's time we occupied it again.

In New Zealand and Australia, whenever someone dies in a road accident or is killed in a public place, people establish informal shrines made of flowers, candles, crosses, and memorabilia left at or near the site of the incident. Asian immigrants often display religious shrines in their shops and homes. For some reason, as Christians, we are less willing to take our faith outside of our church buildings.

I'd like to see church communities and individual households become more aware of how we can provide sacred spaces for the public around us. While these can be made available for meditation and reflection at any time, sacred spaces curated by Christians can be particularly meaningful in times of communal crisis. When tragedy strikes your community, when world events create a universal sense of loss or confusion, it might be appropriate to open the front doors, porch, gate, or side door of your church building, and set up a meditative prayer space with seating, a tray of candles, and peaceful music. Allow people to come and go as they please twenty-four hours a day for a few days. It might also be appropriate to set up something on a riverbank, a public park, the pavement, a front yard, or anywhere else people will gather as they deal with the crisis at hand.

These sacred spaces aren't about evangelism or recruiting new people for your church. They are about providing a place and opportunity for people of all hues to engage with the questions and mystery that they sense but usually can't describe or name. They are meant to acknowledge and facilitate the grieving and reflecting process. This is installation- and stations-based space that is in and for the wider community. People come and go as they please. Nothing is offered or expected. No interaction is sought. It's a chance to just be.

I participated in a church-hall-based space that was established when the Iraq conflict was escalating. The hall was directly accessible from the street without going through any other spaces. The space consisted of a row of seats facing a small table with a television running images of the war and a sign inviting people to sit and reflect, then light a candle as a symbol of their desires to see the war end. Are thoughts about wanting war to end as valid and efficacious as prayers for the same? I'm not sure there is any difference.

During the massive and sometimes-violent G20 protests in downtown Melbourne, the police asked all inner-city churches to close and lock their doors and have security guards stationed nearby to ward off violence. We chose to keep our doors open (the only church that did), have a barbeque on the front steps, and sit around chatting with people from all sides of the protests as they stopped to eat. The foyer space of the church had a blackboard and candle tray for embodied prayers, small crosses to hold and be reminded of injustice, and a video loop with background music playing. For us, this was what it looked like to be the church in a time of crisis and confusion.

Creating this sort of sacred space requires a reeducation. We find it difficult to do anything other than take our usual Sunday worship and reproduce it—or elements of it—in a public place. We have to ask, "What do I want to say?" and work from there to figure out how to create a sacred space in the situation and setting that has been presented to us. Anything less is less than God expects of us.

Creating pop-up sacred places in public spaces recognizes God at work in all places and seeks to cooperate with the Spirit. These spaces will generally not follow an order of service like those I have suggested should be used in community worship, but most of the principles and concepts discussed do apply.

Large-Scale Sacred Spaces

Another subset of guerrilla worship or curated sacred spaces in public places is large-scale public art installations and stations-based work. These fit well with the current trend in Western cultures for pop-up retail and event spaces. Shops, festivals, and bars arrive overnight, often in unlikely places, and always for a short time frame. The events described below are very carefully crafted spaces that required months of preparations and not inconsiderable financial cost. Despite this, they only lasted for a short time. Events of this scale are not the only option, but perhaps seeing what's possible will spark ideas that work for your community.

Two outstanding examples will help illustrate this context of worship.

Trees at the Meteor: Hamilton, New Zealand. Curated by Dave White, Artist and Community Worker.

A few years ago, Dave White gathered a group of Christian and non-Christian young people and young adults in his community and invited any individual or group in his city to enter a Christmas tree competition. There were five categories for entries:

1. Kiwiana[69]: Tree that reflects what it means to celebrate Christmas in Aotearoa[70]-New Zealand. Pine tree provided.

2. Avant Garde: Tree exhibiting innovation, novelty, and originality. Entrants are required to construct the tree itself and any decorations.

3. Recycled: Tree and decorations made predominantly from recycled materials. Pine tree available if desired.

4. Pasifika/Maori: Tree that reflects some aspects of Pasifika or Maori cultural experience. Half round timber "pou"[71] will be provided.

5. Stencil Art: Judges will be looking for an insightful critique of contemporary Christmas culture in Aotearoa-New Zealand, as well as an innovative use of the stencil medium. A plywood tree form will be supplied. [72]

On payment of a $15 entry fee ($10 for students), participants were given a tree (with the exceptions noted above) and a set of Christmas tree lights. Prizes were awarded for each category, and there was also an overall winner and a people's choice winner. The trees—all fifty of them—were installed in the space—a publicly run gallery hired for the event. Once the judging was completed by outside judges, the space was open to the public for a five-day gallery event. Several thousand people paid the $5 entry fee to gaze with wonder at the fantastic, the gorgeous, and the bizarre trees. A café with live music performances gave people a chance to linger and talk and allowed people a space to gather after. The café area included stilt-walking angels, a nativity scene, a carol-singing choir, a social-justice response by way of a World Vision project, and children's activities.

Even by my broad definitions, this was not a worship event. But it was certainly a sacred space where people were engaging, usually unwittingly, with aspects of the biblical Christmas story, and certainly in a positive community-building experience provided by a clearly Christian group. The Spirit of Christmas was palpably present. This was a group doing something positive for their wider community and asking nothing in return.

A Christmas Journey of Peace: Christchurch, New Zealand. Curated by Peter Majendie.[73]

This project is perhaps easier to recognize as guerrilla worship. Conceptual artists, Peter and his wife Joyce, have been doing large-scale, church-based, and public worship installations for a decade. *Christmas Journey* is the latest in a run that has repeatedly covered Christmas, Easter, and Pentecost. This series has seen stations inside shipping containers, in every room of a church, and in numerous public places. Like all installation art, this process has evolved over time. Neither this concept nor its execution has happened out of nowhere.

At five o'clock in the morning, on a day about a week before Christmas, twenty men and women gathered in the darkness of an inner-city public park in downtown Christchurch and awaited the arrival of the first truckload of what would be 1,000 large bales of straw. They arranged the bales single height to form a huge St. Paul's Labyrinth[74] shape. (This was designed by British alternative worshipers in 1999 as a shape made from straight lines, and, thus, easier to scale and set out, and to allow spaces within it for stations to be set up.)

The stations within the labyrinth path allowed people to engage with the following concepts in a reflective space:

- Peace at home
- Peace at work
- Peace in the community
- Peace in the world
- Peace with God
- Peace with myself
- Peace in the economy
- Peace with the earth

For this installation, the stations were all large-scale. There was a mirrored plexiglass "confessional" people could enter and write a postcard to themselves describing anything they wished had never happened, or anything they needed to confess, let go of, move on from, or be at peace with. (You'll recall the impact this had on the police officer mentioned earlier.) These postcards were displayed publicly on a wall, and some—with their authors' permission—were scanned and uploaded to a website during the event.

At another station, a large barbed-wire enclosure had images of people suffering poverty and injustice attached to the wires. Visitors were invited to attach a cable tie as a prayer for those who suffer. At another, small ceramic tiles were provided for people to write a thought or prayer for peace in their native language. These tiles were then attached to wooden box "towers" that spelled out *PEACE*.

Even the publicity for this event was meant to draw people into a new kind of experience. In the weeks preceding the installation, Peter and his crew crafted 5000 small figures out of driftwood and plastic eyes, and attached tags that read, "Take me to the Peace Labyrinth," along with the time and location of the event. These stick people were distributed through schools, cafés, workplaces, shops, and churches over several weeks and were an integral part of the experience. People who turned up without one were given one as they entered the labyrinth. They were invited to add their figures to the growing community of stick people around the nativity hut in the large open center of the labyrinth.

This sacred space was open twenty-four hours a day for five days. More than 3000 people came through. Many recorded their sacred experiences in the comments book.

Both of these pop-up worship installations or sacred spaces were inspired by and based on art forms. Installation art can provide a foundation for creatively approaching any work of guerrilla worship.

Although I have never done anything with it, I am inspired by the installation art of the European guerrilla-arts group that constructs works of art in parking spaces. Group members arrive early enough to find two adjoining parking spaces, park their truck in one, feed both parking meters, and quickly construct their well-planned installation in the other. They then drive away and leave the installation, returning when the meter expires to remove it all. It has possibilities for sacred spaces. I'd love to set up a parking space with grass and a park bench during the Christmas rush downtown, or use it to draw attention to a justice issue.

A guerrilla worship event builds on the same principles and values as any other worship event but requires a lot more work and planning than a community worship event. More consideration needs to be given to the overall environment and context and how the event will be perceived by the public who don't necessarily share your values. For an outdoor space, there are many more practical considerations like local government regulations, electricity supply, and weather to think through than if it was curated in your church hall. More importantly, a lot more time has to be spent in planning and pondering what the installation will look like and the ways you are wanting to engage with people and people with you. Answering the "What do I want to say?" question becomes very important. And it's followed by "How do I say that?"

These are not events that can be thrown together at the last minute by a single person. Collaboration and a division of tasks is vital. Collaboration is also important because no one person can be strong at everything. If your strength is in art, you are likely to need someone who is good with theology and language to ensure that the stations have engaging content. The reverse is also true. Having others around you also helps to carry you through the difficult and doubt-filled times that often come and, most importantly, means you won't be packing out on your own.

Perhaps the most significant issue, and the most often neglected in these settings, is to carefully work through the language you use in advertising, in installation and station notes, and in any speaking at the event. This is not the place for the language of Zion or the King James Version of the Bible. Reframing of the whole event needs to be done with the non-Christian target audience clearly in mind. Thoughts, words, drawings, or candle lighting don't have to be called "prayer" or "confession" for them to be such to God.

The examples described earlier raise the question of how individualistic or collaborative curating is or should be. The sheer size of these projects meant that a team was involved at most stages. As the curator's task is to hold the event together, it is difficult, though not impossible, to actually curate the event collaboratively even if the planning is done with others. It is necessary (if our values mean anything) to have a variety of people participating and supporting the event even if it is community worship. Collaborative planning can work well, as can collaborative participation in curating elements of a worship event, but ultimately the curator needs to take charge of the process. To do so collaboratively requires a high level of trust and confidence between those working together.

For several years, I had the great joy of curating collaboratively with another person. It was a wonderfully satisfying and inspiring experience made possible only because we knew each other well, were both low on ego, had slightly different strengths, and had absolute confidence in each other. (This confidence was not only in each other's abilities but in our mutual commitment to seeing each event through from planning to packing out.) The reality is that, while we worked closely on aggregating and pruning, when it came to curating the actual worship event, one or other generally took the lead.

TRANSITIONAL WORSHIP

This category covers everything that doesn't fit under community or guerrilla, which doesn't mean it is of lesser value or significance. It tends to be moving way from community worship and toward guerrilla worship. Again, it's an arbitrary category into which I put worship events or sacred spaces curated in schools, hospitals, prisons, and at various Christian camps and conferences. These are places where there are likely to be people at all points along the spirituality continuum, but the space itself is seen primarily as a Christian or at least religious setting. The work I do for World Vision staff in conferences sits here, as would much of what Marcus Curnow[75] does through SEEDS in

Melbourne and what Cheryl Lawrie does in carparking buildings.[76] On a good day, the community worship event taking place in the local park could be considered transitional worship, along with an outdoor baptism carefully reframed for the setting.

There is likely to be very little difference in the role of curator in community or transitional worship settings. Often there will even be a similar order of service or list of elements, but they might look different to those in a church setting. I find it useful to think of most worship events I curate in terms of the same outline or pattern of worship elements. The context determines how much emphasis will be given to one over another and what will be pruned.

A Service on the Order of Service

As an example of transitional worship, below you'll find the eight stations curated by Arthur Amon at his church one Sunday a few years ago. Although they were used in a community worship context, they could easily have been guerrilla, and are at least in the transitional category. They are also examples of well-written, albeit quirky, stations that are contextualized for the community for which they were intended. This is what appeared in the bulletin:

The service today, brought to you by Arthur Amon

This morning's service arises from the idea that if we don't always follow the same order of service, it will help us to appreciate the things we normally do more and also give us a break from them. It is also dedicated to the idea that morning tea is an integral part of our worship together. Let us continue to worship God as we eat and drink together. (If this is a bit minimalist for you, there are also some stations you can wander around at your leisure or stride to purposefully.)

Children are most welcome to remain, and there are activities set up that they can apply themselves to, or avoid as they see fit.

Station One: Morning Tea

Think about morning tea as an act of worship. If you want to, you can try and have morning tea with this in mind. Maybe it will affect your conversation, listening, decisions about who to talk to, and so on. Make yourself a cup of tea in the way you like it.

Optional activities: Talk with someone you don't know or don't know very well. Talk with someone you'd like to know better.

Station Two: Offering

Consider the offering and giving in general. You could think about these verses if you wanted to: 2 Corinthians 9:7, Micah 6:8. [Both passages were written out in the insert.]

If you have come prepared to make an offering, you can make it here.

Station Three: The Introvert's Corner

Feel free to spend as long as you like reading a book from the church library. You don't have to talk to anyone if you don't want to.

Station Four: Children's (and any interested adult's) Activities

Coloring, pipe cleaner bending, and so on, on a fishy theme.

Station Five: Fish Display

Today is the first Sunday of Creationtide in the church calendar, straight after the vernal equinox. The theme of this station is the devastation we are wreaking on the oceans of the world. It is a call to action that a single Sunday morning in September will not adequately answer. Feel free to avoid it if you want to eat fish in blissful ignorance.

Station Six: Prayers

Feel free to light a candle at any time for a prayer need you know about, or if you feel comfortable doing so, ask someone to light one for *you*.

Station Seven: The Hypothetical Antibillboard Billboard Project[77]

Here is a chance to exercise your imagination and get a sense of ownership of the project. What kinds of things would you like to see on it?

Station Eight: Music

Listen to some New Zealand music, loosely about fish or the sea.

I have reported this service as it is a clear example of transitional worship. Even in the very creative and open-ended setting of this church community, it was a long way from their usual patterns of worship. But it still took place in the church building and was at the usual service time. The stations occurred in what would otherwise be known as the sermon slot. A number of people who wouldn't normally attend church did so that day out of their relationship with Arthur the curator.

Lingering With Intent: Staff Day of Prayer, World Vision Australia. Melbourne

This was a ninety-minute worship segment for about 500 diverse people in the context of a day at a large conference center. After a ten-minute introduction to the theme, attendees were invited to explore a series of stations. The title and theme of this event was inspired by a scene in the movie *Smoke*. Early in the movie, there is a scene where a character named Paul is looking at a series of photo albums. He is moving through them so quickly that he is admonished to slow down, or he will miss what they are about. We took this as the setting for the worship: slowing down to listen and hear what God was saying. Lingering with intent.

This conference center is set on a large piece of land, and we used every acre as participants moved between four or five main buildings. Some stations were inside, some outside. The journey motif added to the sense of lingering. Because of previous bad experiences with unhelpful weather, we set up most of the main stations indoors and linked them with a series of ten outdoor stations along the paths likely to be taken between buildings. These stations were made up of umbrellas with meditations and thoughts on them. They allowed people to linger even if it was raining.

We also included thirty camera stations that were visible from one station to the next and drew people around the large outdoor areas. These were stand-alone model cameras constructed from takeout-food boxes and mounted on trios of garden stakes. The intention was that people would sit at the chair behind them and linger. Reflect. Slow down. They picked up the underlying theme of lingering that was presented through the introduction and movie clip.

The umbrellas were the surprise success of the day. In a meditation adapted from the video artist Seyed Alavi, the station notes read, "Imagine you have the opportunity to speak on national television, but are limited to a single word. Consider further that after you say your word you must take a vow of silence. In essence this word would be your last. Write that word on a cue card and attach it to the umbrella." Other umbrellas replaced the words "on national television" with other kinds of audiences—colleagues, the Australian Prime Minister, children living in extreme poverty, the local church community, your great-grandchildren.

It was a delight to see people standing around the umbrellas in groups discussing what they would say. Several hundred cards were filled out and hung. The only complaints I had were from people who didn't have enough time to get around to all the umbrellas, even though we'd told them they shouldn't expect to engage with every station.

An equally simple station was a large printout of a biblical passage chosen as the focus for reflection. The text was spaced out, so people could write or draw their comments and questions about the text around and in between the text itself.

We included a confession station in which people were asked to consider this question as they wrote out their confession with highlighters in a black light room: "Linger. How has the past year been for you? Think about a situation in your past year/month/week/

day that you would like to undo, or to have another opportunity to do differently. Words. . .thoughts. . .actions. . . . When you are ready, write or draw your prayer to God for forgiveness, and for another chance. Run it through the shredder [we provided a shredding machine] and step out into the light."

Of the stations created for this event, three had a total of thirty-five variations people could engage with, several more occupied a whole room each, and another was a group viewing of a looped short film. So there were enough stations not to cause people to have to wait in lines, but not so much variety that people were left confused about the options.

The station that took the longest to build, cost the most money, and which I liked best, drew a very mediocre response. It could be described as a failure. It involved eight large cardboard tubes suspended vertically from the ceiling. People were encouraged to lay on the carpeted floor and look up into the tubes. Inside each tube was a backlit word for reflection. People wanted to stand up inside them rather than lie down. Most people passed them by altogether. I should have made the tubes wide enough to get inside and also provided cushions. I didn't think about people with bad knees or backs. It didn't work well at all. But I still like the concept a lot and will use it again in a modified form.

This event is a good example of the collaborative versus solo curation process I referred to earlier. My role as curator involved working both alone and collaboratively. In the early stages, I looked for a theme and possible biblical text. I also answered the question: "What do I want to say?" As that all became clearer, I talked with two other people and regularly ran my developing service and stations notes past them. This was the aggregation stage. We did this by e-mail and phone from different parts of the country. So it was collaborative, and yet I retained the final say. There was no attempt to be consensual.

I find this a very good way to work as it speeds up the otherwise lengthy alternative process of many face-to-face meetings and bowing to the lowest common denominator in order to keep everyone happy. Pruning was within my role as the lead curator. The process worked because of the high levels of trust and confidence we had in each other. Without that, there would have been little inclination for any of my cocurators to wade through twenty pages of stations-in-progress notes and comment at length on what they thought worked and what didn't. It was a wonderful process to be part of. My collaborators traveled internationally to come together for several days at the venue to fine-tune, set up, deliver, and pack out.

This transitional worship event followed a regular pattern of worship. It began with a call to worship in the form of a candle-lighting ritual and responsive reading, and ended with a corporate benediction once we were all back together. The introduction of the theme, the movie clip, and the connected biblical texts served as a sermon before we dispersed. Confession, communion, meditation, and other responses came concurrently by way of the stations. Underneath a very different looking worship event were the elements of a very ordinary order of service.

I hope that you are able to see that grasping a few principles and having some new vocabulary and language when you think about designing worship can enable you to produce a worship event or sacred space that is beautiful, strong, creative, and engaging. There is no magic formula; neither is there a style of worship that is the answer to your prayers. Rather there is a different perspective to be gained from standing and looking at your familiar worship from a less familiar place. You may find the place you stand to look at the worship event described in the next chapter is even less familiar.

11

Contemporary Stations of the Cross

The ancient and traditional devotional form of Stations of the Cross has undergone a significant revival in the last decade. Many churches now offer various forms of the devotion during Holy Week or Easter. Using the Stations of the Cross in a worship event or sacred space, regardless of the context, in the twenty-first century is a significant example of the technique of reframing described earlier. As such, transferring it to present day settings with integrity requires some understanding of its history and original purpose.

Like the term itself, the broader practice of Stations of the Cross arises from a convergence of various paths. The sites associated with events in the life of Jesus, particularly the events leading up to his death, naturally became very significant for his followers once he was no longer with them. Pilgrimages to these sites began in the early centuries of Christianity, perhaps immediately after the death and resurrection of Jesus.

By the Middle Ages, retracing Christ's journey—from his arrest in the garden through to his death on Calvary—at the "actual" spots those events took place, was the practice of many and the desire of many more. A trip to the Holy Sepulchre, the tomb of Christ, in Jerusalem was determined by priests and confessors to be a penance for a serious sin. Of course, this required lengthy and expensive travel by ship and on foot to and through a region that was even more dangerous then than it is today. To overcome this difficulty and make this devotion more accessible, the Holy Sepulchre was replicated all over Europe by various church organizations and monasteries. Markers were placed around and outside the church to suggest the events that took place on the way to Calvary.

At the same time, soldiers coming home from the Crusades (1095–1290) began building tableaus in their hometowns in Europe to remind them of the places they had seen in the Holy Land. This devotional aid became known as the Little Jerusalem. The first clearly defined set of stations outside of Palestine was built in the fifth century, but it wasn't until the fourteenth century that the practice of creating sites that sought to replicate first-century locations became widespread and accessible to the masses.

In 1493, a most remarkable combination of architectural, artistic, and devotional endeavor came together at Varallo in the Sesia River valley north of Milan. A Franciscan friar who had recently returned from looking after the holy sites in Palestine established himself at the new Varallo convent among the sparse population that lived in this rugged, mountainous area. He decided to build tableaus depicting the stages of Christ's Passion on the mountain behind the convent. Pilgrims who exerted themselves with the climb up and around this 500-foot high mountain would be rewarded along the way with access to an expanded set of Stations of the Cross housed in small chapels.

Each chapel contained detailed, lifelike—and life-sized—combinations of sculpture, painting, collage, and relics re-creating in minute detail the gospel events that lead to Christ's Passion. The first building developed was the Holy Sepulchre that copied exactly the dimensions of the Jerusalem sepulchre, which tradition held to be the original tomb of Christ. Each building housed elaborate paintings along with clothed, life-sized characters carved in wood with moveable limbs.

Following the preaching and teaching of the Passion story, pilgrims moved up the mountain visiting the numerous chapels, but they were not able to move at their own pace nor to wander freely. Franciscan friars experienced in guiding pilgrims in Jerusalem now directed the responses of pilgrims in the New Jerusalem. Yet they were encouraged to interact specifically and physically with the tableaus. The original chapels had no separation between props and pilgrims, and a multisensory engagement was sought.

As pilgrims looked at the scenes and mingled with the elements of the tableaus, they were encouraged to recite the Lord's Prayer or the Apostle's Creed. They were invited to use their imaginations to hear the sound of the hammer nailing Jesus to the cross, to smell the spices in the tomb. At the Nativity, they were encouraged to kiss the feet of baby Jesus, join the procession with the Magi, take the baby in their arms at the Purification. A widely read devotional text from the early fourteenth century encourages pilgrims to "kiss the beautiful little feet of the infant Jesus who lies in the manger and beg His mother to offer to let you hold Him awhile. Pick Him up and hold Him in your arms. Gaze on His face with devotion and reverently kiss him and delight in him."[78]

Over the centuries, these tableaus became increasingly stylized and miniaturized until we end up with the small carvings and paintings that every Roman Catholic and many other churches have on their sanctuary walls today. These are also reproduced in booklet form. What started out as a risky journey to the Middle East, from which a pilgrim might not return, has become a devotion that can be followed without even getting out of bed. This perspective moves us away from the realistic representations of the *sacri monti*, and toward the contemporary stations presented by Christian artists today.

Still, any use of the Stations of the Cross in our culture needs to be based in an understanding and respect for the long tradition of this form of worship. It is not a casual affair, nor is it one to be used lightly. It can, however, be made current with careful and thoughtful reframing and curation.

STATIONS FOR THE CHURCH TODAY

The number and titles of the stations have varied greatly over time, and it wasn't until the 1450s or 60s that the term *station* was first connected to this pilgrimage (reputedly by William Wey, an English pilgrim to the Holy Land). In fifth-century Bologna there were only five stops on a *via crucis*, but in other places there were more than thirty stations. In 1731, after 400 years of popular use of the Way of the Cross as a devotion, Pope Clement XII Corsini fixed the number at fourteen and gave them the titles that continue to be used today:

1. Christ is condemned to death by Pilate
2. Jesus is made to carry the cross
3. Jesus falls for the first time
4. Jesus meets his blessed mother
5. The cross is laid on Simon of Cyrene
6. Veronica wipes the face of Jesus
7. Jesus falls for the second time

8. Jesus speaks to the women

9. Jesus falls for the third time

10. Jesus is stripped of his garments and receives gall to drink

11. Jesus is nailed to the cross

12. Jesus dies on the cross

13. Jesus is taken down from the cross

14. Jesus is laid in the sepulchre

You may notice that several of these stations depict events that aren't found in the biblical story. A surprising update to the Stations of the Cross occurred in 1991. During Holy Week that year, Pope John Paul II took part in the Way of the Cross at the Coliseum in Rome. There he broke with tradition by omitting the three falls of Jesus, Jesus' precrucifixion encounter with his mother, and the incident of Veronica wiping Jesus' face. These five traditional stations were replaced with events from Jesus' final days that are recorded in the gospels. Now the Roman Catholic church has officially sanctioned a set of stations that are entirely drawn from biblical incidents.

John Paul II's list that year read:[79]

1. Jesus prays in the garden of Olives

2. Jesus is betrayed by Judas

3. Jesus is condemned to death by the Sanhedrin

4. Jesus is denied by Peter

5. Jesus is judged by Pilate

6. Jesus is flogged and crowned with thorns

7. Jesus carries his cross

8. Jesus is helped by Simon of Cyrene

9. Jesus encounters the women of Jerusalem

10. Jesus is crucified

11. Jesus promises to share his reign with the good thief

12. Jesus is on the cross with his mother and disciple below

13. Jesus dies on the cross

14. Jesus is placed in the tomb

There has been some modern debate over the lack of reference to the Resurrection of Christ, and some liturgists and theologians add it as a fifteenth station, while others see the sepulchre of station fourteen, from which Jesus was resurrected, as sufficient stimulation to meditation. I have always resisted the sometimes-strong pressure from Christians to include the resurrection in the list of stations I use as I feel Protestants are too keen to move quickly over the pain and suffering and get to the joy and renewal part of the story. This was typified by a high-tech, very expensively produced Good Friday service I attended where the service began with the congregation singing the hymn "Up From the Grave He Arose!"

Our Easter Stations installations always closed on Easter Saturday, before the resurrection. In the installation notes for Station 15, we included an invitation to return to the same building on Sunday and celebrate the resurrection of Christ. We set the scene for the Sunday service by not removing all the art but simply clearing some spaces around it for people to gather, making some open space, and removing the covers from the windows to allow in as much light as possible. Thus the resurrection was celebrated among the reminders of Holy Week. Easter Sunday is given a context by being celebrated among the remnants of the stations.

Contemporary Stations of the Cross

The variety of presentations and uses of the Stations of the Cross by churches over the last decade could fill a whole book. But I'd like to describe for you two that I think will spark ideas for how your community might incorporate this ancient tradition into a Holy Week worship experience. Both are full Stations of the Cross, art-installation-based, sacred-space experiences curated for the general public, rather than art exhibitions on Easter themes or smaller-scale local church community projects.

Stations of the Cross: Contemporary Icons to Reflect on at Easter, Auckland, New Zealand. Curator: Mark Pierson[80]

This event ran for about ten years at Cityside Baptist Church. My original concept, floated in a letter to fourteen Citysiders in January 1997, was to follow a labyrinth pattern with the stations somehow located within it. Any form of creative art would be acceptable, other churches could be invited to view the art, and we could meet at Galbraith's Ale House afterward to reflect on the experience. A meeting over lunch a few weeks later garnered enough support to proceed, and the installation opened on Maundy Thursday—less than six weeks after the first pitch!

I had not developed the model of worship curating at this stage, nor was I asking the question, "What do I want to say?" We were a new church plant, and I was looking for ways to use the gifts of artists who were arriving on our doorstep. It was a very basic intuitive process I worked through to find a way to connect these artists with something that would have a public-space outcome.

Origins

That first year we removed all the furniture and pews from our very small worship space and lined the walls with shiny black plastic. Art was hung on a central dividing wall constructed for that purpose, and the works were lit with candles and table lamps sitting on the floor. The art included a wider variety of media than almost any year since—three televisions running two video loops, a single television and loop, seven televisions in a "cross" stack running two video loops, walk-through tunnels, interactive face wiping, oil on canvas, calligraphy, mixed media, and a cartoon. The installation was widely advertised and 370 people turned up over the several evenings it was open. Verbal feedback about the experience was overwhelmingly positive.

The basic concept remained unchanged over the following years. The artists, many of whom had no formal training or any previous experience producing art, were charged with reflecting on the biblical story assigned to their station and coming up with a way to help others interpret and reflect on that text. Sometimes I included the traditional nonbiblical stations, but generally, and particularly in recent years, I stuck to the biblical story more closely.

Artist and station selection

Other than the first year when we were all scrambling to get something together in such a short time, I started the organizational process early. Each October, I distributed among the congregation a printed list of the fourteen stations and biblical texts selected for the following Easter. The list also included tasks beyond the actual art, such as soundtrack, promotional graphics, photographer of record, and preparation of installation notes. Any Citysider could contribute by signing her or his name alongside a station or task.

There was no censorship, and neither the content, style, nor medium of the pieces was checked beforehand in any way other than to ensure adequate space and technical services such as electricity were available. As famous art curator Walter Hopp said of the artist's brief for an exhibition, "My only requirement was that it had to fit through the door."[81]

Control of the content came from an awareness of the relationships and the range of sensibilities within the Cityside community, as only people from within our community were invited to contribute. We had several hard discussions as a community about what people saw as acceptable and what wasn't. This was not written down and was not legislated, but all artists were aware of the story they stood in—they were part of a community that looks back and looks forward.

The only parameters set for artists concerned the size of the work and the intention of the artist.[82] As curator, I did not see the art until it arrived to be hung or placed in the space. The event was as much about providing a platform for Cityside's artists as it was about providing a contemporary re-mediation or reframing of an ancient sacred art form to help people interact with the gospel story. While many artists produced work for a number of years, and some booked a specific station more than a year in advance, every year was open to anyone in the church community. Unlike the stations installation described below, generally artists participated as individuals, although they were always part of the wider Cityside community and dialogue about the biblical text, and the stations were constant among the community.

Station Design

The design required that the Cityside auditorium was stripped of all furniture and the considerable wall hangings and art. Black fabric (although we had experimented with silver paper and black plastic previously) generally lined the walls. The space was designed and walls constructed to form a pathway around the art—this design varied considerably from year to year. We also set up a separate enclosed area for reflection and communion. The art was then placed and lit by individual spotlights, and an original soundtrack ran in the background. Originally, the space was open from six o'clock in the evening or midday until midnight, Wednesday to Friday of Holy Week. In 2003, to cope with increasing numbers of participants, we extended the hours to include Saturday.

Concept and Principles

While the concept remained the same over the years, the design, promotion, and curation improved and developed with each installation. The number of people coming through rose from 370 to more than 1200. The budget rose from $500 to $6000. Funding came primarily from trusts and private individuals. The church itself did not contribute funding directly but picked up incidental costs such as photocopying and administration.

This financial independence from Cityside Baptist Church was primarily the result of my personal feeling that all Cityside projects should be run and sponsored by those with a commitment to them rather than being funded by the church as a whole. My previous experiences of church had often included expensive projects dreamed up by an individual or small group who then expected the church to fund their proposal, usually on the strength of a simple majority vote.

This issue was complicated further when the vision to be funded came from the senior pastor. The unequal power relationship can tend toward abuse and gives ideas that originate with employed staff priority and value above those of pew sitters. I preferred to give individuals the opportunity to be involved financially if they wanted to, but didn't expect them to be. I have long been committed to the concept that if I believe God has given me a vision for a project, then God will also provide the funding required rather than my expecting someone else to fund my ideas, whether they like them or not.

Our presentation became a well-known and anticipated event each Holy Week in Auckland. There is something special about building a presence in the city from an ongoing repeated event. It builds depth and expectation. Up to sixty Citysiders were directly involved in making each project happen. Many other groups and churches around New Zealand and across the world are now doing similar work, often in more creative ways than I had done. One year I corresponded with a large nondenominational church in Los Angeles that staged a wonderful set of sculptural stations around an outdoor promenade between their buildings; an ecumenical group in Glasgow used a Baptist church building for their event; a Christchurch couple opened their highly interactive stations by taking over all the rooms in an entire large suburban church building; a woman in Seattle curated a very interesting Stations of the Cross in a Quaker context; another inner-city Auckland church made its first foray into an art exhibition on the Easter theme; an alternative-worship group in Dunedin (New Zealand) offered an Easter exhibition in a community gallery space. And all of those in the same year. Many more have followed.

Space Design

Our space at Cityside was relatively small. The building is basically a ninety-year-old traditional wooden church that has been badly messed up by various remodeling efforts. In other words, the space for this event was nothing special. The stations would be set up in the rectangular, level-floored sanctuary space, a room about forty feet by twenty feet with a fifteen-foot ceiling.

One year, the general concept was to create a gloomy, New Zealand-style garden of Gethsemane into which the icons of the last week of Jesus' life would be placed, leading participants on an engaging journey through that narrative. We stripped the sanctuary of all its contents, including wall hangings. We then hung a continuous strip of matte-black fabric (weed-control cloth) along the walls. Windows behind and above this level were blacked out before being covered with cloth. The environment created for the art involved twenty-five people using eight wheelbarrows and more brooms to move in fourteen tons of beach sand and spread it four inches deep over the entire floor. (A plastic sheet underlay went in first.) This took less than ninety minutes.

We set up timber stands for the fourteen stations, creating a path winding through the space as we did. We hauled in 150 native trees, bushes, and grasses, and, using corrugated iron, built a waterfall in one corner. The art was installed and then lit with individual low-voltage halogen lights.

Just off the main installation space, we created an area for relatively private individual reflection on the experience. This space, lit only with candles, had an artificial-grass floor covering and a range of black fabric-covered couches to sit on. Bread and wine were available for self-service communion beneath a large suspended crucifix, borrowed from our neighborhood Roman Catholic church. At the opposite end of the building, an exit space was created using black cloth curtains and lit by handmade, sculptural lamps. We added original ambient electronica soundtracks to both the main space and the exit space.

People entered up the usual entrance ramp from the street and into the small foyer of the building adjacent to the one used for the installation. Here they were welcomed and given a set of installation notes, a brochure of the related biblical texts (produced specially for the installation by the Bible society), and invited to take off their shoes and socks and carry them in a jute bag. These bags were manufactured by Bangladeshi women who made them as an employment alternative to prostitution.[83]

After walking through a short transitional corridor, people entered the main installation space. It was down a few steps, giving people something of a grandstand view of the installation from the small landing before moving down and onto the sand. At this point, the ambient soundtrack was audible, and the journey around the stations began. The reflective space could be accessed at any time down several steps off the opposite end of the main installation space, although not immediately visible due to the trees and shrubs. Visitors from previous years would expect some kind of reflective space in this area.

After moving around the stations for whatever period of time they wanted and backtracking as often as desired, visitors exited up an internal ramp through a dark area lit only by a series of small neon cross lamps and into the main exit space. Here they could purchase their jute shoe bag and, thus, support the Bangladeshi women, make a donation, fill in a response form, replace shoes and socks, read related literature, or just wait for friends before finally passing back through the entrance foyer and onto the street from which they had come.

This setup was considerably more sophisticated and complex than those of previous years. Until then, the art had generally just been placed around the outer walls of the emptied and blackened space and a soundscape provided. Each year had seen an increase in sophistication from the previous one, such as from lighting with bed lamps to low-voltage halogens. This was partly due to financial constraints, but more so because I chose to work within reasonably tight financial boundaries that forced us to think carefully about how we used our resources. There was also an inevitable ramping up of expectation by participants and a desire to make each year's presentation "better" than and different from the previous year.

The individual artist brief has always been to reflect on the biblical text relating to the segment of the Holy Week story selected; to interpret that personal encounter with the story in any media of the artist's choosing (within certain given parameters of space); and to make that interpretation available to the public in order to encourage reflection on the Holy Week events, during Holy Week.

Evaluation

The overwhelming highlight from this installation was the very positive comments from a large number of people about the impact it had on them. Approximately 1100 people came through the "garden," and the 120 comments in the book recorded some significant, even life-changing, encounters with God through interacting with our remediation of the Easter story.

I noted that the use of the newly available extended building and the design of the installation worked very well. I wondered if this increased space and subsequent lack of congestion actually encouraged more chitchat between visitors. I often found groups standing talking to each other in the space (usually while their children played in the sand!). Interestingly, this almost never happened in the exit space, nor the reflective space. The garden itself turned out to have quite high levels of ambient noise with the waterfall, station one soundtrack, and the four-source main soundscape all contributing.

My own criteria for evaluating this event were applied before we ever opened the doors to the public. Stations of the Cross at Cityside Church was always about providing a brief, a deadline, curation, and a public to whom this group of creative people could present their efforts. It was about developing the artists before it was about putting on a show. So if all the artists met their brief and deadlines, I considered that a success. If people turned up to experience the environment and engage with the stations, that was a bonus. We were working to develop the artists before we were working to engage with a public. For that reason, any evaluation was primarily about how well the artists had worked, cooperated, and met the brief.

Standards

That year, I thought the general standard of art was slightly higher than in previous years, although it still included a wide range of skill levels. Two of the pieces became finalists in the Fifteenth Annual Wallace Art Award (these are the biggest and longest-surviving art awards in New Zealand), and one piece was purchased by the James Wallace Charitable Arts Trust for its collection.

I received three letters of complaint about Stations. None from people who attended. Responding to one man who had written me a letter complaining about the Catholic influence (that is, Stations of the Cross) threatening the Baptist Church, a member of the Cityside congregation contacted him and brought him to the installation. A good conversation ensued.

No artists were paid for their time or materials.

This installation was firmly based in a church setting, and it's processes and outcomes were closely connected to the values of that community of faith. Attending it could be described as an outsider being invited in to someone's home. The Stations of the Cross installation I want to describe next is more like being invited to a street party.

Stations of the Cross: Easter Art installations, Hamilton Gardens, New Zealand. Curator: Dave White[84]

In the provincial city of Hamilton, Dave White started with a loose group of Christian and non-Christian young adults he was working with in his community. He invited them to produce a piece of art either individually or collaboratively and installed these in a huge, derelict, concrete-sided factory downtown. The finished works covered fine art to ghoulish installation (an over-bath shower running "blood"). In his perceptive and inimitable stream-of-consciousness way, Dave told me in an e-mail:

> I had a hunch that Stations of the Cross could be missional. And I needed a good hunch because my multimedia presentations, my coffee bars, my door knocking, my Christian t-shirt, my altar calls, and tract-giving pursuits were less than pretty. Little return. Not good. Slim evangelical pickings. It could be missional, even though still largely an attractional project, because art still has currency in the marketplace. Good art does not dictate to the viewer, good art invites, good art offers, good art does not force the mind of the viewer. To my untrained mind, you could allow the viewer a space to view, and trust that the Spirit would move, and therefore a non-Christian brave enough to view an art exhibition with a religious theme would be rewarded by quality art, the Jesus narrative—postmoderns love a good story— and the presence of the Spirit. My conviction was born out of my personal experience of the Stations at Cityside. I found the Easter story framed in my

cultural context gripping, real. It was aesthetically pleasing, stimulating. I had a conviction that artists worshiping Christ, illuminating Christ through visual images, images and installations formed through a Kiwi worldview, is a very significant experience both for viewer and the artist.

Dave and his community have done the Stations of the Cross for three years in a great theater space in town and four years in a public garden space. He went on to say, "My conviction that art, and Scripture, and narrative, and journey make for a significant medium rings true every year as feedback from the participants comes in. With fifteen stations, for every personality type, for every viewer's artistic bent, for every person something about at least one station will move them—sometimes deeply."

Dave's brief to the mostly young artists in his community has remained constant: to "create stations—multimedia art installations— that Dave believed would resonate with youth culture that breathes with images and art and appeal to a growing hunger for mystery and spirituality that longs for connections with the past." As Dave and his community plan the event now, they deliberately work in an environment of collective dialogue.

The process begins with all the artists for a given year writing down what they envision for the stations. At each subsequent meeting, the group discusses three of the stations. These conversations are no-holds-barred confrontations and reflections on the ideas, art, theology, and perspectives being suggested. After many weeks and many meetings, the group, having decided what the content of each station will be, then decides who will curate each station. It's a highly collaborative, ego-busting process. A revolving core of five or six artists is involved regularly, and several others contribute for a single year.

After a few years in their theater venue, Dave and his team nego-tiated with the Hamilton City Council to use the huge public gardens as their venue. This meant the works had to be much larger and weath-erproof. It also meant a lot more work in terms of installation. To top it all off, the city council required that the gardens be open for tourists each day, so every night at ten o'clock when the Stations closed, all the works, lighting, sound, and cabling had to be packed out, then rein-stalled from six o'clock to eight o'clock the next evening. But they did it—fifteen stations, a café, and a reflective area fully imported and as-sembled in two hours, open to the public for two hours, then disman-tled and stored in ninety minutes, for seven nights. After seven years, Dave took a sabbatical.

The Hamilton stations event was more obviously a pilgrimage than the Cityside event. People lined up outside the gates and entered in groups where they were given a historical explanation of what the Stations of the Cross are about, and then given their individual MP3 player and flashlight and set on the path. Through headphones they could hear a commentary about each of the stations—not an expla-nation as much as an interaction with each station. Viewers walked a mile or more around the fourteen stations and ended up back where they began, at a café and response area.

The stations included fine art and sculpture as well as interactive installations and street art: a man in a rooster suit wandering around asking people, "Do you know Jesus?" and squeezing a box that made a rooster crowing sound; the garden of Gethsemane, where two rows of raised stadium bleachers—each seat with a sign on it inviting peo-ple to "Wait for me while I pray"—looked down on grass turf where a goblet lay. Sometimes two or three works were located at each station.

Often Stations would challenge or raise issues in the culture at the time. New Zealand has an appalling record of child abuse. In one horrible case, a toddler was hung on a clothesline and beaten by three family members. So one year station 6—Jesus is mocked and beaten—was a rotating clothesline with baby blankets of different sizes and shapes hanging from it, some covered in blood. There were pictures on the walls behind of New Zealand backyards and children's toys on the ground.

In the course of five years, the number of attendees grew from 400 to 3000. Comments from participants were always very moving. One night I followed a group of local art critics through several stations. They were not Christians but from their conversations were obviously able to engage in significant ways with the story and the stations because the art provided an entry point. Three months after Easter, Dave wrote, "My previous not-so-God-fearin' boss came through stations and still has the program on her fridge. Why? Who knows?"

STATIONS IN A WORSHIP FRAMEWORK

While both of the Stations of the Cross installations described here deliberately aimed to have viewers engage with the biblical story and hopefully also with God, there was no attempt to convince the viewer that the medium or artist didn't exist. There was also no attempt to pretend that what was presented with the installation was in any way a reproduction of the original setting of the story of Jesus. (Most of the stations at both venues were conceptual and interpretive anyway.) The fact that it was happening in a wooden church building in downtown Auckland or in a public garden in Hamilton was not disguised. But it could be argued that the desire of many viewers to encounter God in this multisensory retelling of the story does in fact elicit an emotional response that produces the effect of immersion in the viewers.

Station notes are important to each of these projects. The usual information about artist, materials, station number, and title is supplemented by a brief comment from the artist. Some artists balk at doing this, but I insist on it. Not everyone is art literate, and some short comment about what inspired or prompted the artist to produce the work she did can be helpful to the viewer accessing the work and meeting God through it.

Some of the more abstract works, while presented in a context of the wider Christian story and more narrowly restrained by the station they are representing, were completely open to interpretation by the viewer. The viewer was invited by this lack of prescribed content to interact directly and have an authentic emotional response to the work. Knowing the biblical story was not critical to that response. Yet curators of contemporary Stations of the Cross installations should expect that God will engage with people and vice versa.

Anthropologist Victor Turner applied his understanding of liminality and communitas to the experience shared by random strangers brought together by a journey, in particular a pilgrimage.[85] In the same way liminality can be applied to an encounter with these Stations of the Cross, that, by the nature of participants traveling to the venue and then walking from one station to the next, can also be understood as a pilgrimage, even if those participating are unaware of the connection. God can enter the liminal moments created.

Don't be overwhelmed by these two examples of the Stations of the Cross. Both had small beginnings and developed over a number of years. They illustrate just two ways of many that these stations can be done in church-based and public-space-based settings; by individual artists and by collectives; by trained and untrained artists. In neither case is the event primarily about the quality of the art, although that always has to be of a standard appropriate to the anticipated audience.

It is about the community of faith participating in engaging with the biblical story and producing a response in some art form. That's where the main benefit lies. As I said before, I always felt that if no one turned up to go through the Stations installation, it would still be a success as it was primarily a project for our own church community. Anything else was a bonus.

Having said that, I need to sound a note of warning. If you have no artists in your community, and no particular interest in or engagement with artists and the arts, you shouldn't curate a Stations of the Cross event for the public. To do so would be inauthentic and lack integrity. Both the examples above grew out of the creative space within their communities and were appropriate to the time and space they were in. You may find that a more internally focused response has more integrity for you. A community day of clay, art, junk sculpture, paper-making, songwriting, poetry, or flower arranging based on the stations might be better. By all means, use the stations as a focus for the creative skills of your community, but keep it in-house. This has huge benefit for those involved as they engage with the biblical story through a creative process. It's very participatory and more closely aligned with many of the other values I have promoted for worship. Besides all that, you will avoid a lot of criticism!

More to the point, you will avoid offending people. Unlike most other forms of curated space, a Stations installation has plenty of room for upsetting people. Offending someone with a piece of art on public display is very easy to do. It's better for offense to come as the result of art that has been carefully thought out by its creator than from the well-meaning but uninformed efforts of someone who doesn't really care for art or understand the artistic processes. I recently curated an Easter installation with a group from a large church. The pastoral leader insisted on seeing every piece of art in advance, so he could ensure it was "acceptable." Only he knew what this meant, and he was unable to communicate his criteria.

This form of censorship raises several issues, none of which are resolvable by anyone except those involved in the installation. The need to censor is about control and power. To my mind it says more about the insecurities of the pastoral leader than it does about anything else. I understand that no pastor wants to be criticized by anyone in the congregation, or to have to answer for someone else's art. I understand it, but I don't support it. If you need to censor, you are saying to your artists that you don't trust them or know them, that their gifts aren't God given, and that they are not really part of your community. If you need to censor, you are saying that the arts are so powerful they scare you and you want to tame them, and that you are so insecure you need to bring them down to your level. The art you offer will reflect this and always be insipid, bordering on the bland, and never reach beyond the already well-converted. If you feel the need to censor for any reason other than quality or integrity of the work, keep asking yourself what is going on inside you, where those feelings are coming from, and why you need to do this. If you think the reasons you come up with are good enough, then okay, do it.

Finally, I think that curating the Stations of the Cross year after year is the worship event most worthy of Ashleigh Brilliant's prayer in "Pot Shots Number 2588": "Lord, help me to meet this self-imposed and totally unnecessary challenge."

12

Inspiration and Resources

I think it's sad that often only very unusual worship gets labeled *creative*—even more sad that only a few *people* get labeled creative, leaving most people to think they aren't. Certainly some people are more creative than others, but far more people can curate creative worship than you might think. This means of serving a community shouldn't be restricted to a special group or individual. In my experience, anyone can make a creative contribution to a worship event. It depends on how we nurture that kind of participation and value it in our churches.

Worship that calls for trucking a ton of crushed ice into a sanctuary lit with black light isn't necessarily any more creative than having a congregation tear out newspaper headings as prayers. Neither are primarily about creativity. Both are about curators figuring out ways to help their particular communities engage God with heart, soul, mind, and strength during a particular worship event.

For years I had a slogan on my study wall that said in effect, "The courage to be 'down' is necessary for creativity." Creativity has often been associated with depression and melancholy. Munch and Picasso come to mind. But I've come to see that this isn't a fair coupling. My guess is that there are as many very happy creative people as there are melancholy creative people. The melancholics just make more fuss about their situation! We complain and look for sympathy and support. But creativity doesn't require depression.

American writer Robert Fritz has a refreshing take on creativity. He slaughters some sacred cows (like saying that laziness is the mother of invention rather than necessity and that brainstorming is counter-productive) along the way to describing what he understands creativity to be. He says that creativity comes out of the tension between a current reality and a desired outcome.

The process of wanting to get from one to the other produces creativity. So in his view creativity requires some dissatisfaction with the status quo but not necessarily melancholia.

To interpret his language, creativity is letting your mind find equilibrium between a desired outcome and a current reality. Creativity operates in this structural tension, in this area of dissatisfaction. The greater the difference between the two, the greater the creativity required to bridge the gap. The clearer the idea you have of what you want to create and the more accurate your view of the current reality, the easier it is for you to be creative. [86]

I like that approach. It takes creativity out of the magical basket and puts it into one that can be grasped, understood, and worked at. As musician Charles Mingus has reputedly said, "Making the simple complicated is commonplace; making the complicated awesomely simple, that's creativity." Over time, as we gain experience and increase our knowledge of solutions to bridging that gap, we become more creative. Increasing creativity is actually an expanding repertoire of previously experienced possibilities that we connect in increasingly networked ways. Playing and fooling around with combinations of possibilities is, therefore, a vital part of developing our creative muscles, as is reflecting on our failures.

We human beings tend to look only at end results and overlook the process. We see someone doing something so creative that it leaves us speechless, and we are in awe of it. We want to be like them, able to produce similar stunning outcomes. But we forget that what we are looking at is the result of many years of that person gathering creative outcomes and combining them in new ways to provide new solutions. We also face the temptation to be consumers of the creativity of others. There is nothing wrong with taking an idea from somewhere and using it in your worship setting. But make sure you go through the process of making it your own and reframing it to fit your community and context.

Creativity will always involve risk and the possibility of failure and criticism. All the more reason to know the answer to the question: "What do I want to say?" The most important knowledge you can have is self-knowledge. You must be self-aware enough to understand your motives, humble enough to be able to apologize, confident enough to stand by your decisions and intuitions, and empathetic enough to know when to let go of your great idea for the greater good of the worship event. Fear may be your greatest emotion—fear of criticism, of failure, of offense, of sinning, of the unknown, of embarrassment. These are all reasonable fears! Rather than try to overcome or suppress these, I prefer to heighten my awareness of them. Then I can choose which I will listen to. They can all be muses that speak to me in different ways and make me aware of why I am making a certain choice in my curation. God can speak through my fears as well as to them. Ruth Duck wrote:

> It is difficult to trust one's own creativity, to remain open to images and symbols emerging out of one's journey with the Spirit. Many of us have learned to discount our own perceptions, our own truths,

especially if we have grown up in families where we were abused and silenced or in schools where every peg was supposed to fit in the same size hole. We may have internalized social values that deny a woman's right to shape the language of prayer, or we may have believed the myth that real men don't develop their creativity. Perhaps, too, we have accepted values that keep us too busy to cultivate a relationship with God or to listen to truths emerging within us. Finding our own creative voice, surfacing our own images, experiences, and perceptions can be difficult.[87]

Your greatest resource is yourself—in particular, your self-aware self. It is imperative to both the creative process and the curating role that any curator be committed to a process of self-growth and what we used to call sanctification—becoming more Christlike. One of the more useful resources I have found helpful in this process is the unlikely titled *The Naked Now: Learning to See as the Mystics See* by Richard Rohr. In very gentle yet clear ways, he helps the reader to work through issues relating to failure, fear, success, ego, personal transformation, and many others relevant to the position of the worship curator.

ARTISTS AND THE CHURCH

Sadly, the church is not always affirming of the creative voice. But I see that changing as churches become aware of the crucial role art plays in the church. The next move has to be toward an understanding that it is not the art itself the church needs to value, but the artists. It's the artists who are part of the worshiping community. They are the ones who need avenues for expressing their gifts and access to engagement with God through those gifts in the same way those with singing or musical roles do.

If you decide to pick up some of the principles I have written about, one of the problems you may have in your church is with your leadership team—particularly if you are accountable to a senior pastor. Without his or her intentional and declared support and permission, nothing new of significance will happen in your church worship. This is particularly true if you wish to involve artists other than singers, musicians, and dramatists in the worship life of your church. It is entirely understandable that a senior pastor and leadership team have the needs of the whole congregation in mind. That is how it should be. But that shouldn't mean always deferring to the loudest critic of any project.

I believe the major contribution a senior pastor can make is that of standing between the artists and the community and defending the perspectives of both. A significant role for anyone in leadership is to hold open the spaces in which other people may respond to God's call in some way, and to ensure a safe, open, and empowering atmosphere is maintained in those spaces. This is not easy to do, and I know from experience the rush of stomach-churning emotions that flood through me when an artist comes up with a public work that I know is likely to offend someone. It has taken me many years of asking God to give me insight and wisdom into my own responses to be able to deal with that.

To have integrity for both the church and for artists in that church, the interaction between them must be about artists rather than about art. It's the artists who are part of the worshiping community and it's they who need to have expression for their gifts, and access to engagement with God through those gifts. Most churches are more interested in getting a recognizable painting of Jesus to hang on the sanctuary wall than they are of an abstract interpretation of an artist's engagement with what God has done in their lives in allowing Jesus to die on the cross. It's an important distinction and why I don't think many churches will actually allow their artists to interact in any significant way with their worship. It's simply too dangerous for most senior pastors and leadership teams. It's too open ended. It's not measurable. It's not containable in a neat box. It hangs over the edges, and the lid won't fit on. The moment an artist gets beyond simple description and into the depths of interpretation, there is the potential, even likelihood, of the "c" words. Controversy. Conflict. No pastor likes to experience them. I certainly don't.

Pastors will sometimes defend theological minutiae to the death (sometimes theirs and sometimes their congregation's), but an artist who causes controversy among those who pay the senior pastor's salary? Too often pastors will allow that person to be hung out to dry. I regularly hear stories of this happening. While I can understand it, and have faced the temptation to do so myself, it's wrong. This is exactly why we need artists contributing to the life of our churches—in worship and other ways. They bring insights and challenges that unsettle, and question in ways that nothing else can. It's in this opening up, this liminal moment, that God can speak to us, particularly to those of us who are more likely to encounter God through visual media than through spoken words.

Even when the pastor does support artists, there are often strong people in leadership who will react badly at the first whiff of oil paint they don't understand. Will the senior pastor be willing to stand in that gap between the artist and the leader, or the artist and some vocal members? That's the role of the pastor in my opinion. Whether or not the pastor takes up that challenge, the artist needs to recognize that the worship wars are real. People resist change, and, whether as pastor, curator, or artist, you need to not be naive about the opposition and criticism you will face. A pastoral tenderness often goes with being a good curator, so you need to look after yourself. Getting inspired can be dangerous to your mental and spiritual health, but if you've read this far you probably can't help yourself!

It is also worth checking that you haven't created an imaginary opposition for yourself. Sometimes we use what we imagine people will think about an idea as a reason to not pursue it. In order to protect ourselves, we decide that we shouldn't follow through on a particular idea or response or station or installation. We do it by telling ourselves that Mrs. Jones or Little Billy wouldn't like it, so we won't do it.

There are many and complex reasons why we protect ourselves in this way. They need figuring out and dealing with if you are to become the curator God is calling you to be. Sometimes working on your relationship with people you think are likely to be your biggest critics is the best way forward. In my experience, many of these people— whose ability to criticize hurtfully was very real— became my strongest supporters. It's much harder to publicly criticize someone with whom you have a good relationship. By keeping up a good relationship with these people and keeping them informed about what I am planning and why—which sometimes means framing it in language they can relate to—they are more likely to give me the benefit of the doubt and to trust me, even when they don't fully understand what I am wanting to do. After all, as curators we want to enable everyone in our communities to engage with God.

FINDING INSPIRATION

If we are going to do more than drag and drop someone else's worship event into our communities, we need to find ideas and resources. Back in chapter 3, we talked about the aggregation process—finding artifacts and ideas that inspire worship. For me, this process involves being immersed in contemporary culture. Attend art installations and read about installation art; go to movies—any genre; listen to music and attend concerts; visit design stores and read architecture magazines. Walk the aisles of cheap novelty shops, art supply stores, and hardware stores to see what's available. Go to events you don't think you'll like. Attend art gallery openings and artist talks. You will rapidly come to see all of these places and events in a new light and find they are feeding your creativity and filling you with more possibilities for worship than you can possibly use. Go to original sources as often as possible—I would discourage you from reading books about other churches and from looking to other churches for your inspiration.

Inspiration index

I also find that simply thinking about materials helps spark new ideas for me. With that in mind, I want to share with you a list of items that inspire me. This is by no means an exhaustive list, but I hope it gets you looking at ordinary objects with the eyes of a curator.

> **water:** flowing; steaming; ponds lined with black plastic to make black water; floating candles or corks; dissolving ink writing; origami boats with messages or words on them; waterfalls that fill communion cups; hand washing and foot washing; ice blocks— handheld, cross shaped, large to scratch on, filled with small objects, colored with food coloring, lit up, melting.

> **sand:** candle trays, large pile of sand to hold candles, cover a tabletop for candles; footprints that rake away; write in it and smooth over; large quantity to

walk in; haunting Eric Bibb track, "I Want Jesus to Walk With Me"; Godly Play, place objects in the sand.

umbrellas: open, closed, open and closed, upside down, upright, for hanging things on, with lights inside or lit outside, to project onto, to fill; cocktail, sun, beach, golf, backyard umbrellas.

grass turf: bringing the outdoors inside; garden of Gethsemane; tactile; holy ground, take off your shoes.

fire: Are there alarms and sprinklers? indoors and outdoors; wok or brazier; burning papers written or drawn on; light and heat; Scriptures about fire; burning bush—soak pumice in flammable liquid; fire gel; Peter denies Jesus around a fire; fire purifies, destroys, clarifies; fire extinguishers choke off air supply.

incense: prayer; grains; bowl or thurible; self-help or censer; toss into wok fire; needs lead time to get charcoal hot.

paper shredder: shred what you draw or write, leave on floor, burn, walk on; walk shredder around or stationary; confession.

clothes line: hang Christian-year festival labels in order as a teaching method; newspaper headlines as prayers; timeline.

cardboard boxes: Christian year festivals written on them to put in order; timeline; plinths for station materials; paint them; collapsible and storeable; signs

THE ART OF CURATING WORSHIP

painted on, lights within and cutouts; peek holes
with objects within; objects or text on inside, put
head in to see; personal confession booth.

mirror: tiles or sheets, small or large; fragmented or
whole; distort, reflect; write on with soap or pens and
wipe off; under water need surface smooth and still if
to see clearly; mirror film bends.

black light (ultraviolet light): cotton fabric, fluoro paint
and highlighter pens, some laundry powder, shaving
creams, white paper glow under it (fluorescent paint
holds for a few seconds an image made with laser
pens or projected onto it.); tubes, lamps, spotlights;
needs dark environment for good effect; stick dipped
in glue then laundry powder makes a pseudocandle.

projections: ambient, didactic, wallpaper; screen—wall,
walls, umbrellas, people, boxes, sheets, translucent
fabric—multiple layers (garden-plant frost cloth
works well and is very cheap); soundtrack or silent;
looped or linear; rear or front projection; number and
placement of screens—front, back, sides, center.

labyrinth: hand draw Cretan or borrow canvas Chartres
labyrinth; put stations into bulges or around outside
edges; make with stones, petals, candles, flour, wool,
sand, shells, pasta.

soundtrack: sound effects, recorded, live, lyrics,
instrumental, moody; "The Lament" by Tanya
Sparkes, *The Passion* soundtrack, electronica; check
for crescendos; background or foreground; lyrics in
handout or on screen.

Those are some of the ways I think about how I will create responses and vehicles for content in worship events I curate. When it comes to inspiration for aggregation, I'll let movie director Jim Jarmusch have the last word:

> Nothing is original. Steal from anywhere that resonates with inspiration or fuels your imagination. Devour old films, new films, music, books, paintings, photographs, poems, dreams, random conversations, architecture, bridges, street signs, trees, clouds, bodies of water, light and shadows. Select only things to steal from that speak directly to your soul. If you do this, your work (and theft) will be authentic. Authenticity is invaluable; originality is nonexistent. And don't bother concealing your thievery—celebrate it if you feel like it. In any case, always remember what Jean-Luc Godard said: "It's not where you take things from—it's where you take them to."[88]

THE FUTURE

What I have described above and throughout this book is only a beginning. We need to think much more creatively and deeply about how the church operates in the world and come up with better solutions than we have so far found. In some ways, I fear all my talk about worship is just shifting the deckchairs on the Titanic—it makes for a more comfortable ride as we sink. But what if we were to not treat church services like a fast-food outlet that people get in and out of as quickly as possible with a spiritual takeaway?

Imagine what church could become if we offered a curated, stations-based worship space that was open for extended periods of time for people to come and go as they wished or were able? This would be a space that provided guided possibilities but no locked-in time frame. What if the worship space was open for several hours, or even twenty-four hours a day, seven days a week? You could participate at any time that suited you, or arrange to meet friends for worship before or after an outing as well as at advertised corporate gathering times.

There could be a café, a chill-out space for conversation, a laundromat, maybe a spiritual director or pastoral staff attached. Perhaps the main space has an entry room where you can hear the recorded biblical text read and some "sermon-like" introduction to the text. After this, you enter the main installation space and respond by way of the stations there.

Corporate worship on Sunday at ten o'clock in the morning still happens, but it's in the curated installation-worship space. A regular order of service is followed, with the stations being the response time. The stations installation stays up for the following week, or even two weeks. The time and money put into it gets a much better return than setting up for thirty minutes in a single service.

This approach raises questions about the balance between corporate and individual worship, and whether there needs to be a balance. Would individuals worshiping at different times but experiencing the same curation still be church? Just how liquid can church become before it ceases to be church? And do the answers matter?

This kind of continuous, slow-worship space could easily be offered by any existing community of faith—a community offering both gathered and scattered worship events, both solid and liquid church in Pete Ward's description. It's not uncommon for inner-city churches to open their buildings for tourists to drop in. Why couldn't an interactive sacred space be available in the same way?

I believe this worship-as-art-installation is the future of corporate, public Christian worship in the West. Worship in the future will involve either a single major or several minor art installations curated as interactive stations of response to and engagement with the biblical story. These installations will be located in church buildings, clearly recognizable as such (missional, transitional, or guerrilla worship spaces will likely be located in other venues), and be accessible twenty-four hours a day or at least for extended times daily. These worship spaces will allow both the gathering of communities at various set times and the transient individual, family, or other group who wishes to engage with God in some way at a time that suits them. There may or may not be other activities of spiritual formation taking place in the same space or other spaces in the same building during these extended worship times.

These installations will draw their inspiration and language from the vibrant world of installation art and, hopefully, begin to hold their own in that space as valid works in the genre. The church desperately needs artists and theologically educated pastoral leaders willing to collaborate as they curate these worship installations. Perhaps when they do, the art world will experience some redemption too, and the church will be able to grow worship in the soul of its culture.

Arts writer Graham Coulter-Smith, having described the usual experience of visiting an art gallery and being kept at arms length or more from all the works, goes on to describe a very different gallery experience. It is instructive for a worship-installation center such as I have suggested above:

> Then I walked over to the Ars Electronica Center. They don't even call it a gallery let alone a museum. It is an extraordinary art gallery not only because it is devoted to interactive art, but because it is noisy. The

> highly visible orange-coated personnel are not there to stop you touching the exhibits they are there to help you touch them. . . . The inveterate art lover will experience something akin to culture shock or a panic attack. . . . Some of the pieces are obviously designed for children. . .though there are enough pieces that possess sufficient aesthetic sophistication to make even the aesthete's visit worthwhile."[89]

I hope you have begun to see the relationship between installation art and worship, and life and culture and worship, and the possibilities of curated worship. I also hope you have been inspired to try some new methods and processes in your worship curating. With all this new language under your belt, you can now describe yourself as a worship curator rather than a worship leader. You can say of yourself as I do, "I curate structured and ambient events and spaces that offer people the potential for liminal moments of individual and corporate engagement with the Trinitarian community of God. I am an artist whose medium is worship."

May God be with you.

Notes

1. WHY CHANGE?

1 For an excellent summary of this history, see *Alternative Worship in the Church of England* by Paul Roberts (Cambridge, U.K.: Grove Books Ltd., 1999).

2 St. Louis: Chalice Press, 2003.

3 See chapter 7 in *Experience God in Worship: Perspectives on the Future of Worship in the Church from Today's Most Prominent Leaders*, ed. by Michael D. Warden (Loveland, CO.: Group, 2000).

4 From Carol Wade, "Stories of Resurrection: Traces of God in New Community," published in Yale Institute of Sacred Music's *Colloquium Journal*, Volume 2, Autumn 2005, and online. http://www.yale.edu/ism/colloq_journal/vol2/wade3.html (accessed April 9, 2010).

5 Mike Riddell, "Deep Currents of the Heart," *The Rite Stuff: Ritual in Contemporary Christian Worship and Mission*, ed. Pete Ward (Oxford, U.K.: The Bible Reading Fellowship, 2004), 76.

2. FIRST THINGS FIRST

6 "10 Types of Emerging Church That Will No Longer Upset Your Grandfather," *Tall Skinny Kiwi* (December 31, 2009), http://tallskinnykiwi.typepad.com/tallskinnykiwi/2009/12/index.html (accessed 8/14/2010).

7   http://www.donnadinsmore.com. See note in text, on p. 22.

8   *Foundations of Christian Worship* (Louisville, KY: Westminster John Knox Press, 2007), 207.

9   Graham Cray and others, *The Post Evangelical Debate*. (London: Triangle, 1997), 35.

3. CURATION: THE GLUE THAT HOLDS IT ALL TOGETHER

10   Andrew Lórien, Cathy Kirkpatrick, Mark Pierson, and Mike Riddell, *The Prodigal Project* (London: SPCK, 2000), 62.

11   Brian Doherty, *Inside the White Cube: The Ideology of the Gallery Space* (Berkeley and Los Angeles: University of California Press, 1986), 65.

12   Curator job was posted on the website, Prospects: The UK's Official Graduate Careers website, http://ww2.prospects.ac.uk/p/types_of_job/museum_gallery_curator_job_description.jsp (accessed February 16, 2010).

13   *Random House Unabridged Dictionary with CD-ROM*, 2nd ed., s.v. curator.

14   Mike Shatzkin, "Aggregation and Curation: Two Concepts That Explain a Lot about Digital Change," blog of The Idea Logical Company, Inc., http://www.idealog.com/blog/aggregation-and-curation-two-concepts-that-explain-a-lot-about-digital-change (accessed October 20, 2009).

15   Ibid.

16   A *station* is a place in the worship space where items are placed and people invited to move around and interact with them. Chapter 8 explores stations in depth.

17   The Princeton Review, "A Day in the Life of a Curator," http://www.princetonreview.com/Careers.aspx?page=1&cid=48&uidbadge=p (accessed February 14, 2010).

18   Suzanne Page quoted in *A Brief History of Curating*, ed. Hans Ulrich Obrist, (Zurich: JRP/ Ringier), 236.

19 J. Randy Taraborrelli, *Madonna: An Intimate Biography* (New York: Simon and Schuster, 2001), 19.

4. A NEW LANGUAGE FOR WORSHIP: APPLYING THE PHILOSOPHY OF CURATION

20 Mike Riddell, Welcoming Liturgy, *"It's Worship Jim But Not As We Know It": an Emerging Worship Course*, 2000. Reprinted with permission of the author

21 Steve Collins, *A Definition of Alternative Worship* (2005), alternativeworship.org: Changing Church in a Changing Culture, http://www.alternativeworship.org/definitions_definition.html (accessed August 15, 2010).

22 Quoted in Ruth C. Duck, *Finding Words For Worship: A Guide for Leaders* (Louisville, KY: Westminster John Knox, 1995), 3.

23 Pete Ward, *Liquid Church* (Peabody, MA.: Hendrickson Publishers, 2002), 72.

24 http://twitter.com/JesusQueries.

5. A NEW LANGUAGE FOR WORSHIP: DESCRIBING CURATION PRACTICES

25 Quoted in Michael Frost, *Jesus the Fool* (London: Lion Hudson Publishing, 1994), 71.

26 Author and original source unknown. It appears on numerous websites.

27 For inspiration see http://www.gi-inc.org (click on "enviromental projections") and http://worshipvj.com.

28 August 3, 2003.

29 Quoted in Ruth C. Duck, *Finding Words For Worship: A Guide for Leaders* (Louisville, KY: Westminster John Knox, 1995), 103.

30 From their album, *Swamp Ophelia*.

31 Email to author. In "A Collage of Beauty: An Interview with the Agents of Future," Brent Thomas writes about Todd and his processes.

Holiday at the Sea (blog), Jan. 20, 2009, http://www.holidayatthesea.
com/?p=37 (accessed August 16, 2010).

32 Ibid.

33 "Praying with Candles," on his blog for August 29, 2009, at http://
wonderfulawful.wordpress.com/2009/08/29/praying-with-candles/
(accessed August 16, 2010).

34 Larger candles can be polished with a nylon stocking, and if you use
a snuffer to extinguish a candle, you are more likely to keep the wick
standing straight up and not have trouble lighting it next time. Before
starting a new, larger pillar candle, first trim the wick to about 1/4 inch
to reduce smoking and encourage a more even burn. A new candle
should be burned one hour for every inch of diameter and allowed to
cool before burning for long periods. This encourages the wax to pool
evenly rather than develop a crater in the center. Recycle candle ends
into new candles by melting the wax in a double boiler and pouring
into a mold. Use boiled natural string as a wick.

35 You can make a thurible out of an empty tin can with chain attached,
but incense works well in any fire-safe source such as a small grill or
wok. Don't put the container directly onto carpet, especially nylon
carpet, or a wood surface. Bricks, sand, or pavers underneath work best.

6. A NEW LANGUAGE FOR WORSHIP: BUILDING COMMUNITY THROUGH CURATION

36 Brian Eno, "Ambient Reflections," *Studio Sound Magazine* (U.K.), 1995.

37 Victor Turner and Edith L. B. Turner, *Image and Pilgrimage in Christian
Culture: Anthropological Perspectives* (New York: Columbia University
Press, 1978), 249.

38 Victor Turner, *The Ritual Process: Structure and Anti-Structure* (Chicago:
Aldine Publishing Company, 1969), 95.

39 *Image and Pilgrimage*, 108.

40 See *Secular Ritual* by Sally F. Moore and Barbara G. Myerhoff
(Amsterdam: Van Gorcum, 1977), 43.

41 J. Randall Nichols, "Worship as Anti-Structure: The Contribution of
Victor Turner," *Theology Today*, 41 (1985): 408.

42 This has certain similarities to the idea of "flow" put forward by Mihaly Csikszentmihalyi in *Flow: The Psychology of Optimal Experience* (New York: Harper and Row, 1990).

43 Bob Trubshaw distinguishes between "temporary liminality" and "the more-or-less permanent outsiderhood." See http://www.indigogroup.co.United Kingdom/edge/liminal.htm (accessed June 21, 2010).

44 See William M. Johnston's "Liminality: Episodes of Temporary Marginalization," in *Encyclopedia of Community: From the Village to the Virtual World*, eds. David Levinson and Karen Christensen (Great Barrington, MA: Berkshire Publishing, 2003).

45 *Image and Pilgrimage*, 250.

46 Ibid., 250.

47 Ibid., 251.

48 *The Ritual Process*, 97.

49 Brian Eno, *A Year with Swollen Appendices: Brian Eno's Diary* (London: Faber and Faber Ltd. 1996), 90, 401–403.

7. WHAT DO I WANT TO SAY?

50 (New York: Farrar, Strauss and Giroux), 7.

8. STATIONS: THE NEW ALTAR CALL?

51 *The Catholic Encyclopedia* online at New Advent, s.v. "Way of the Cross," http://www.newadvent.org/cathen/15569a.htm (accessed August 16, 2010).

52 Source unknown.

53 Jemma Allen who works with tations in Hamilton, New Zealand, first drew my attention to this important difference.

54 To learn about Mr. Manovich and his work, see http://www.manovich.net/.

9. CONTEXTS FOR WORSHIP

55 See *Finding Words For Worship: A Guide for Leaders* by Ruth C. Duck (Louisville, KY.: Westminster John Knox Press, 1995) for an excellent overview of the elements of worship. Constance M. Cherry's *The Worship Architect: A Blueprint for Designing Culturally Relevant and Biblically Faithful Services* (Grand Rapids, MI: Baker Academic, 2010) is also useful but much less succinct.

56 I acknowledge the significant contribution Brenda Stone made in editing this worship handbook with me.

57 Some of the material relating to the elements of an order of service first appeared on the self-published CD-ROM, *Fractals: Alternative Resources for Worship in the Emerging Culture.* 2003.

58 Duck, 62.

59 This is my take on Duck's suggestions, 70f.

60 Duck, *Finding Words for Worship*, 71-72.

61 I find *Mass Culture: The Interface of Eucharist and Mission* (Abingdon, U.K. Oxford: The Bible Reading Fellowship, 2008) a useful starting point.

62 *The Cloister Walk*, by Kathleen Norris (New York: Riverhead Trade, 1997).

63 Diane Karay Tripp, *All The Seasons of Mercy* (Louisville, KY: Westminster John Knox, 1987), 86.

64 David J. Bosch, *Transforming Mission: Paradigm Shifts in Theology of Mission* (Maryknoll, NY: Orbis Books, 1991), 391.

10. GUERRILLA AND TRANSITIONAL WORSHIP

65 This is not a typo. The word *guerrilla* can be spelled with one or two "r"s. Smith uses one, while Levinson uses two. That's guerrilla publishing at its finest.

66 (New York: Princeton Architectural Press, 2007), 12.

67 www.christmaslabyrinth.co.nz (accessed August 16, 2010).

68 *Liquid Church*, 78f.

69 *Kiwi* is the affectionate colloquial term used for a New Zealander. *Kiwiana* is therefore anything quintessentially New Zealand.

70 *Aotearoa* is the indigenous Maori name for New Zealand.

71 Maori word for "post."

72 http://www.treesatmeteor.co.nz (accessed August 16, 2010).

73 http://www.christmaslabyrinth.co.nz.

74 http://www.labyrinth.org.uk (accessed August 16, 2010).

75 http://www.seeds.org.au/ (accessed August 16, 2010).

76 http://www.holdthisspace.org.au/ (accessed August 16, 2010).

77 This is a reference to an idea under discussion by the congregation to mount a billboard on the main-street side of the church.

11. CONTEMPORARY STATIONS OF THE CROSS

78 The *Pseudo-Bonaventure*, quoted by Alessandro Nova in 'Popular' Art in Renaissance Italy: Early Response to the Holy Mountain at Varallo, in *Reframing the Renaissance: Visual Culture in Europe and Latin America, 1450-1650* (New Haven, CT: Yale University Press, 1995), 117.

79 Bill Huebsch, *Scripture Stations of the Cross: In the Footsteps of Pope John XXIII* (New London, CT: Twenty-Third Publications, 1999), 1.

80 http://www.cityside.org.nz (accessed August 16, 2010).

81 *A Brief History of Curating*, ed. Hans Ulrich Obrist (Zurich: JRP/Ringier), 22.

82 The intention, or brief, is that the artist will reflect on the biblical text and use that internalized reflection as the inspiration to produce a concrete work of art that will enable a later viewer to interact with the biblical story via that work.

83 http://www.marketplacers.co.nz/ (accessed August 16, 2010).

84 http://www.stations.org.nz (accessed August 16, 2010).

85   See *Image and Pilgrimage*. For more on pilgrimage, see *Pious Journeys: Christian Devotional Art and Practice in the Later Middle Ages and Renaissance*, ed. Linda Seidel (Chicago: Smart Museum of Art, The University of Chicago, 2001), 67.

12. INSPIRATION AND RESOURCES

86   http://robertfritz.com/ (accessed August 16, 2010). For a beautiful and inspiring insight into the creative process applied to worship and for many wonderful ideas to reframe worship, see Mandy Smith, *Making a Mess and Meeting with God: Unruly Ideas and Everyday Experiments for Worship* (Cincinatti, OH: Standard Publishing, 2010).

87   Ruth C. Duck, *Finding Words For Worship: A Guide for Leaders* (Louisville, KY: Westminster John Knox Press, 1995).

88   Jim Jarmusch, "Jim Jarmusch's Golden Rules," *Movie Maker online*, January 22, 2004, http://www.moviemaker.com/directing/article/jim_jarmusch_2972/ (accessed August 16, 2010).

89   Graham Coulter-Smith, introduction to *Deconstructing Installation Art* (Southampton, U.K.: Casiad Publishing, 2006).

Index